# MODERN
# FILM
# SCRIPTS

# BELLE DE JOUR

a film by

## Luis Buñuel

English translation and description of action
by Robert Adkinson

Simon and Schuster, New York

Published by Simon and Schuster
Rockefeller Center, 630 Fifth Avenue
New York, New York 10020
First printing

General Editor: Sandra Wake

SBN 671-20793-8
Library of Congress Catalog Card Number: 75-148384

Manufactured in Great Britain by Villiers Publications Ltd,
London NW5

# CONTENTS

# A NOTE ON THIS EDITION

The present publication is based on Luis Buñuel's original shooting script for the film. The English translation of this version by Robert Adkinson has been carefully revised and checked with the English subtitled print in order to make it as accurate a rendering as possible of the film which the English or American spectator will see on the screen. Significant divergences between the original script and the final screen version are indicated in this script by footnotes and square brackets.

' Buñuel's Golden Bowl' by Elliot Stein is reproduced by kind permission of Mr. Stein and *Sight and Sound*, where it first appeared in Autumn 1967. Andrew Sarris' article on ' Belle de Jour', which appeared in *The Village Voice, Confessions of A Cultist*, and *Film 68/69*, is reproduced by kind permission of Mr. Sarris. ' Two Interviews with Luis Buñuel' appeared in *Cahiers du Cinéma*.

Acknowledgments and thanks are due to L'Avant-Scène du Cinéma for providing us with a copy of Luis Buñuel's original script and to Bargate Films for allowing us to view a print of the film.

# TWO INTERVIEWS WITH LUIS BUNUEL

Q : The admirable thing about your work is its unity of tone, the way in which you preserve your individuality even in films which have been made under the most difficult conditions imposed by the popular commercial cinema.

BUNUEL : Even under those conditions I have always worked in accordance with my own conscience. Not one of my films contains the slightest detail which goes against my moral or political convictions. Within the framework of these requirements I have always done what I have been asked to do.

Q : There are significant differences between the films you have made in Mexico or Spain and those made in France. . . . Your French films seem more polished, made with more resources but apparently less personal.

BUNUEL : In France I have always been offered films which I had no objection to but of which I had not chosen the subject. *La Mort en ce Jardin* doesn't strike me as being very successful, *Cela s'appelle l'Aurore* is taken from a good novel by Emmanuel Robles. The worst of my French films is *La Fièvre monte a El Pao*; during the shooting, Gérard Philippe and I kept asking ourselves why we were making such a piece of rubbish. It was a mystery : neither he nor I knew why.

Q : Which of your films do you think would be likely to be most successful in Spain?

BUNUEL : Chiefly *Nazarin*. But they consider the subject to be taboo. I think nevertheless that a simple, unprejudiced audience would like the film. I don't mean cinema club audiences. I think that in general the Spaniards don't like my films; the logical thing would be to allow them to be shown so that they could condemn themselves. The first two days people would defend them out of sympathy for me, but the third day no one would go and see them.

That would give the world a chance to say : ' Look at the freedom they have now in Spain!' They are secretive films, in which nothing is immediately obvious or apparent. I'm sure that *Los Olvidados*, which is going to be put on there, will not last even two days — 'All that dirt and misery!' — The film will pass unnoticed. I think that *Archibaldo*\* and *The Exterminating Angel* could easily be put on too, but they still consider them taboo.

I've never wanted to demonstrate anything in particular in my films. Didactic or political cinema does not interest me. People really can't accuse me of anything on that score. But whatever I do, they always find some double meaning.

It irritates me when people say that there is blasphemy in *Simon*; I dislike having things attributed to me which I did not intend to say.

Q: What do you know about the new Spanish cinema?

BUNUEL: Very little. I like Francisco Regueiro's *El Buen Amor*. I have a lot of faith in Carlos Saura, although he's a little 'German'; I sometimes tell him that he hasn't enough sense of humour or fun.

Q: How do you see the development of the Spanish cinema in relation to Spanish art and culture?

BUNUEL: Today's youth is an innocent victim of a break with tradition; the umbilical cord linking them with preceding generations has been cut and they are forced to invent everything from the beginning — amongst other things, non-conformism. They have to reconstruct this missing link through books. It's not the same thing at all.

*(Tape-recorded interview with Juan Cobos and Gonzalo S. J. de Erice in Madrid, 15th January 1965.)*

Q: Are you pleased with your latest film, *Belle de Jour*?

BUNUEL: I don't like Kessel's novel at all, but I found it interesting to try and turn something I didn't like into something I did. There are some scenes in the film which I am very pleased with, others with which I'm not at all. I ought to say that I enjoyed total freedom during the shooting and I

---

\* *The Criminal Life of Archibaldo de la Cruz.*

6

therefore consider myself entirely responsible for the result. I am glad to have finished the film and to be able to return to Mexico. I find long shooting programmes tiring and I try to film very quickly. The shooting schedule for the film was ten weeks. I did it in eight weeks because I'd had enough of trying different camera angles and talking a lot of nonsense to the actors. I only used 18,000 metres of film, which is very little, when you think that one can easily use 25,000 on quite a cheap film. I always have the editing in mind when I'm shooting. That way I don't have to do any pick-up shots and the editing is reduced to a process of sticking the shots end to end. I edited *Belle de Jour* in twelve hours and on top of that there was a week which the editress spent on the detailed work. The things which interest me most in the process of making a film are the stages which come before and after the shooting: working out the script and editing. I've worked as an editor in the USA, though admittedly as a rather specialised one.

Q: Will the film be sent to a festival?

BUNUEL: I've no idea. That's the producers' affair. Once the film is finished I take no further interest in it; I don't even go to see it. But it's possible that *Belle de Jour* will be shown at a festival since it's an 'official' sort of film, one which is calculated to bring in a lot at the box office, with good actors. . . . You know of course that it's a pornographic film? No, no, by that I mean a chaste eroticism. Even if the censors look at it differently; I never try to scandalise people, but they sometimes scandalise themselves.

Q: It's your third film in colour . . .

BUNUEL: This time I had a remarkable cameraman — Sacha Vierny, who reconciled me to colour.

Q: Was there some question of your making *The Monk*?

BUNUEL: They want me to do it in France, but I'm no longer interested in the project, I don't like it any more. Everything was ready to go in October, but I wanted to have a month's rest in Mexico beforehand. In fact I stayed there for four months, and when I got back to Paris I found out that the production company had broken up after a quarrel between the two co-producers. They were finally reconciled and took up their old project again, but I wasn't interested in it any more. I like a story at the time of writing it, but after a certain time I don't want to hear any more about it; I don't like it any more and I can no longer make the film.

Q : Did you do a lot of work on the script of *The Monk*?

BUNUEL : Yes, because that's the stage I like best. I have always had a part in writing the scripts of my films, but I always need to do it in collaboration with a writer. I have one fault, and that's repetition, which is why I am no good as a writer, even when it comes to doing a simple letter. It always comes out something like : ' Dear So-and-so, I'm writing to you because my mother has written to me to say that she can't write to you and asks me to write to you . . .' or else : ' There are too many cars on the road. It's impossible to get around by car with so many cars on the road. . . .' All my prose is the same and I usually end up tearing up the letter. It takes me three days to write something which a writer could do in three hours. So we talk and discuss things, and I leave the writing to him.

Q : What do you think, now, of *L'Age d'Or*?

BUNUEL : I like the spirit in which we made it; we were young, and we made fun of the established institutions, the Family, the Church. . . .

Q : Would you say that *The Exterminating Angel* represents for you a return to the spirit of *L'Age d'Or*?

BUNUEL : I know that people have written and said such things, but it's not true. The fact is that I am always the same.

Q : In your first Mexican films, and in particular in *Susana*, you apparently twist the theme round to give it the opposite meaning of that originally intended.

BUNUEL : Yes, that's it exactly, but I'm afraid that the falseness of the ' happy ending ' was not sufficiently obvious. The one I prefer from this period is *El*.

Q : Out of all your films, which do you like the best?

BUNUEL : I've no idea. My tastes are very changeable; today it's one, tomorrow it'll be another. At the moment the one which interests me the most is *The Young One*. When it came out it was a failure; it was very badly distributed by Columbia. That's the way they do things. I wouldn't be surprised, for instance, if they bought Saura's *La Caza* and paid 20,000 dollars for it as easy as scratching your ear, and then distributed it badly into the bargain. That's Hollywood policy; you buy up anything which constitutes a threat in order to avoid competition. But Columbia's policy goes even further than that — it's an artistic policy which consists of buying intelligence in order to destroy it.

But there was another reason for the film's initial failure : at the time it offended both blacks and whites. When the film came out in New York, a Harlem newspaper wrote that I ought to be hanged by the feet, like Mussolini, in Fifth Avenue. The other newspapers didn't even mention it, but the *New York Times* tore it to pieces. In order for people to like that kind of film, the black man must be a hero who saves the white, or vice versa, at the end. But in my film, there aren't any heroes.

Q : What do you think of the Brazilian ' New Cinema '?

BUNUEL : I know *Os Fuzis*, *Vidas secas* and *Black God, White Devil*.* I like those three films enormously, they thrill me. Particularly Rocha's film : it's not very well made, but it's got extraordinary power. Of all the ' young cinemas ' of the world, the Brazilian is the best. They don't have the necessary freedom, but this kind of film will continue to be made, either by them or by others. It's something which exists, which is there. One has only to make an effort to receive it.

Q : Do you like Bellocchio?

BUNUEL : I've seen *Fists in the Pockets* — I don't find it the slightest bit interesting; it's repulsive and far too facile. It's really completely overdone — the blind mother, the retarded brother . . . the son putting his feet on the mother's coffin — it's too easy. . . . While he was at it, why not show him shitting on his mother's head? It's the only thing he spared us.

Q : And Fellini?

BUNUEL : I like his first films a lot. Up to *La Dolce Vita* Fellini was one of the directors whom I found most interesting. Now he's always playing the genius. I saw *Giulietta*; it's worthless. Neither true nor false surrealism, nothing. Those hats . . . what's the point? Technical trickery, nothing but

---

* Directed by Ruy Guerra, Nelson Pereira dos Santos and Glauber Rocha respectively.

technical trickery. Supposing I had to shoot a scene in this room, and you had to open that door and say something in passing to your friend, and then he got up to look for a passport while you went out — well, if I took it in long shot it would be a simple scene with very few movements. But if I did it in medium close-up, you'd have a scene where the camera was constantly on the move. If in addition to that I lit the walls instead of the characters . . . well, that's the opening scene of *Giulietta*. When I begin to ' see ' the technique in a film to that extent, I don't like it. In my own films I always try to make the technique imperceptible. If it's noticeable, then it's no good.

When I saw *Giulietta*, I left before the end and went off to have a Campari. Then I went back to the cinema to watch the people coming out — they all had long faces, like corpses. The cinemagoer is the worst of all. People who go to the theatre or watch sport are different — they talk, argue, get excited. . . . The only people who go to the cinema are those who have got a couple of hours to kill and can't think of anything else to do, or they just want to finger their girl-friends, and who knows what else? I don't go to shows very much, but I like to watch the spectators coming out. And people coming out of a cinema are always as silent as the grave. The fact is that eighty per cent of the films which come out today should never have been made. There are very few films which are really important, or even interesting.

Q : Do you read a lot?

BUNUEL : I don't read much, and when I do I prefer works on biology or history rather than novels. I'm very fond of South American literature. I think Alejo Carpentier is the greatest writer in the Spanish language. *The Lost Steps* and *Explosion in a Cathedral* are two extraordinary novels. So is Vargas Llosa's *La Ciudad y los Perros*. I also like Cortazar, and Miguel Angel Asturias. Though I'm surprised that he's ended up as Guatemalan ambassador in Paris.

Q : Do you like travelling?

BUNUEL : No, not at all. I get a lot of invitations, but I refuse them all. Right now people keep urging me to settle in Paris. I won't — I would be afraid of dying in the process of moving; I don't mind dying, but certainly not while moving house. From now on I shall live in Mexico and only leave to come to Madrid, to see friends and eat and drink. . . . As I said at the beginning of our conversation, I'm sorry I can't offer you a glass of wine, but I'm leaving for Paris in a few hours and the bottles I had left are already packed. I drink a lot, I have ever since I was forty, I'm an alcoholic. I drink two bottles of wine a day, and not only in the evening, I start at midday . . . but so long as my liver holds out. . . . But I don't like getting drunk, and when I feel that I've got to a certain point I stop.

Q : Do you have any plans to make a film in Spain?

BUNUEL : I haven't planned anything since they refused to allow the shooting of *Tristana*. But in fact it's in Spain that I would most like to work. In any case I'm stopping now. I won't make any more films, either in Spain or in France or anywhere else. *Belle de Jour* is my last film.

*(From conversations with M. Torres, Vicente Molina Foix, M. P. Estremara and C. R. Sanz in 1967.)*

# BUNUEL'S GOLDEN BOWL

Most of all, Buñuel wanted to go back to work in Spain again. He had been encouraged by reports that the brouhaha over *Viridiana* had calmed, that censorship there had been relaxed. He returned. Then, after months of preparation, in the summer of 1963, Franco's government refused the shooting authorisation for his version of Galdos' *Tristana*. Later that year, in France, he made one of his finest films, *Le Journal d'une Femme de Chambre*. When shown in Paris, in 1964, it was coolly received. A year later, one of his old pet projects, an adaptation of Lewis's *The Monk*, was finally about to take shape. At the last minute the production company was dissolved, and it too had to be written off. The Hakim Brothers then approached Buñuel to ask him to consider a screen version of Joseph Kessel's novel, *Belle de Jour*. He accepted, and cloistered himself in an ultra-modern building in Madrid with Jean-Claude Carrière (co-scenarist on *Le Journal* and *The Monk*). They finished the script in five weeks. The shooting schedule for this, Buñuel's twenty-seventh film, was ten weeks. He brought it in in eight.

*Belle de Jour* is a masterpiece, technically Buñuel's most accomplished, free-flowing work. It is unique, the only one of his films in which his obsessions, his purity, and his convulsive spirit have all been fully, satisfactorily organised into an architectonic whole. It unfolds so smoothly, with such sustained legato, that there is no chance to catch a breath. *Viridiana* was a step in this direction, the underrated *Journal* a near-arrival. *Belle* is the many-faceted and perfect Golden Bowl, which crowns a life's work. When released in Paris recently, it was greeted with shock, reticence and disappointment by most of the critics for the daily and weekly papers. The great man, tired, deaf, sixty-seven years old and alcoholic (his own admission), now only wants to return to Mexico and rest.

Joseph Kessel's novel, published in 1929, whipped up a fair

*succès de scandale* at the time. Although Buñuel has said of it : ' La novela no me gusta nada,' it is a far from uninteresting book, firmly in the tradition of the French *roman psychologique*, and a precursor of the post-war but already classic *Histoire d'O*. It concerns a beautiful young *grande bourgeoise*, Séverine Sérizy, wife of a handsome young surgeon (Pierre) whom she deeply loves. She has every reason to be happy, but of course isn't. She learns that an acquaintance, a woman of her own class, is working in a brothel. Séverine gradually becomes obsessed by the thought of such a situation, finds out the address of one of these bagnios, and applies for a job there. She only works afternoons from two to five — thus her sobriquet, Belle de Jour. Frigid in the arms of her kindly, well-behaved husband, she is impelled by a masochistic urge for humiliation which leads her to seek out ' rough trade '. Marcel, a doting young gangster, falls in love with her; she soon becomes very fond of him. The devoted hoodlum attempts to kill a friend of her husband who is about to inform Pierre of Séverine's double life. The murder misfires when Pierre intervenes, and it is *he* who is seriously wounded. He recovers, but is paralysed, condemned to a wheelchair. Overcome by guilt, Séverine confesses everything. Pierre never speaks to her again.

Kessel elevated this novelettish plot through a convincing portrayal of the frightening divorce between the heart and the senses. In 1936, Philippe Hériat adapted the book for the stage. The play was rejected by sixteen theatre directors and as many actresses. It has never been performed; with luck, it never will be.

Although Buñuel does not fancy the novel (he didn't like Defoe's *Robinson Crusoe* much either), he stated : ' I found it interesting to try to make something I would like, starting from something I didn't. . . . I enjoyed complete freedom during the shooting of *Belle*, and consider myself entirely responsible for the result.' He took pains with the editing, modifying several sequences in the process — a procedure rare for him. Hindered often in the past by tight budgets, his only inconvenience here was the producers' insidious auto-censorship; several cuts were made by them before *Belle* was sent to the censors.

13

Buñuel's last great film is close in spirit to his first great film, *L'Age d'Or*. Indeed, one of the things in *Belle de Jour* which seems to have bothered people is its fidelity to what can only be called the true spirit of surrealism : not the tacky Surrealism to be found in the moth-eaten commemorative art shows which have popped up from time to time in Paris, London or New York art galleries since the war, but the invigorating, positive, liberating surrealism which marked *L'Age d'Or*, caused riots when that film was first shown, and resulted in its being banned for a generation. The result is more mellow, less overtly aggressive than *L'Age d'Or*, even calm. But it is all there.

Buñuel : ' *Belle de Jour* is a pornographic film . . . by that I mean chaste eroticism.'

The film contains threads of events from Kessel's book. But Buñuel has turned the book inside out, ripped the surface from it, and stitched inside to outside with such invisible mending that much of the time the heroine's real life, her fantasies and childhood memories, are integrated as a fluent story in which past, present, and the merely possible form a solid block of narrative. With her, we fall through trapdoors of consciousness, and then, with relief, fall out of them — but only into new ones.

Buñuel did not like the novel's ending, ' because morality is saved.' The climax of his film is simply the most astonishing ' open ending ' in the history of the cinema. It is the meanest trapdoor of them all (half open? — half shut?), a renewal of the beginning; but once seen, it fastens the entire film into a writhing subliminal image, that of an admirable circular serpent, forever catching its own tail in its own mouth.

The film's motifs are not those of the book. Kessel tells the story of a woman who loves one man with her heart, and a few dozen others with her body — and feels badly about it. Buñuel sidesteps sin and guilt; for him they are obviously luxuries the human race has been burdened with for too long. His film (the theme is far from new to him) tells the story of a liberation from the moral handcuffs of social caste by means of a personal *sacerdoce*, a self-fulfilment.

14

During the main credit titles, an open landau trots down a pleasant country lane towards the camera. Inside it, Pierre (Jean Sorel) and Séverine (Catherine Deneuve) are cosily enlaced. She tells her husband that she loves him more each day. Suddenly, he orders the coachman to stop and his wife to descend. The lackeys drag her through the woods. At Pierre's command, she is gagged, bound to a tree, whipped, etc., by the servants. 'What are you thinking about, Séverine?' an off-screen voice asks. 'About us,' Séverine replies to Pierre. 'We were driving in a landau.' They are in the bedroom of their Paris apartment.

A few days later, at a mountain ski resort, they meet Pierre's friend (Father Lizzardi from *La Mort en ce Jardin* and Monteil from *Le Journal d'une Femme de Chambre*), here called Husson (Michel Piccoli). 'He's rich and idle. They're his two main illnesses,' a woman friend remarks. Returning from her holidays, Séverine learns that a young married woman of her ' group ' works in a clandestine brothel. (Clandestine because Kessel's novel, like France, has been modernised, and *maisons de rendezvous* are no longer legal.) Husson, met one day at the country club, insists on supplying her with details about ' the houses ' he has known. After days of hesitation spent obsessed by troublesome thoughts, Séverine goes *chez* Madame Anaïs (Geneviève Page), and as she climbs the stairs to the brothel for the first time, we come upon a little girl in church (Séverine as a child?) refusing the host. The priest is impatient: 'Get it down you!' Séverine does get herself enrolled in the brothel, and returns that very afternoon to begin work — all gleaming patent-leather shoes Buñuelian style on the stairs.

She is recalcitrant with her first customer, an obese bonbon magnate, but when he and Anaïs get tough with her, she becomes joyfully submissive. One busy day, her list of clients includes a truckling gynaecologist, who has come *chez* Anaïs for the same reason as Séverine — to be humiliated. She cannot cope with him, but is pleased to be manhandled by a huge Japanese who tries to pay with a Geisha Diner's Card. We then see her seated demurely, enjoying the fresh air in an elegant outdoor café near the Cascade in the Bois de Boulogne,

15

where Bresson's *Dames* were wont to meet. (At the next table, too thin to be Hitchcock, is a Spanish tourist, Señor Buñuel, talking business with one of the Hakim Brothers.) She is approached by the one-time leading man of *La Mort en ce Jardin* and *Cela s'appelle l'Aurore* (Georges Marchal). He is wearing no make-up and looks like a weird old French Duke. He asks Séverine if she likes money, and tells her that, indeed, he is a rich Duke. He invites her home for ' a very moving religious ceremony.' They are driven to his château by the two footmen who had whipped her at Pierre's command right after the main credit titles. The Duke dresses her up as his dead daughter, covers her with asphodels, mutters something about ' the inebriating odour of dead flowers,' then disappears under the coffin for a part of the service which the producers removed before submitting the film to General de Gaulle's censor board. When the ceremony is terminated, she is paid for her pains and kicked out into the rain.

One day at the brothel, the Nazarin (Francisco Rabal), who has become a Bolivian gangster, arrives with a young protégé, Marcel (Pierre Clementi). They have just robbed a bank messenger (bringing the profits from the latest Vadim film?) in the lift leading to the Hakim Brothers' office, 79 Champs-Elysées, and are loaded with money to spend on pretty women. Marcel falls in love with Séverine and returns often to see her. She develops a strong physical passion for the hysterical punk, although she still loves her husband.

Marcel discovers Belle's secret identity, invades her home, shoots her husband, and is pursued and killed by the police. Pierre recovers. He is paralysed, has lost the power of speech and will spend the rest of his days in a wheelchair. One beautiful autumn afternoon, Séverine is seen giving her husband his medicine. Then, looking out of the window of her splendid Paris apartment, she sees in the pane the reflection of the pleasant country lane (leading to the Duke's château?) where the landau was driving in the opening sequence. ' I haven't had any more dreams — since your accident,' she lies to Pierre lovingly. She then hears Buñuelian cowbells (first heard in 1930 in *L'Age d'Or* when Lya Lys, on discovering a huge cow on the bed of her splendid Paris apartment, chased the *vache* off the *lit*, looked into a mirror, and saw moving clouds and a vision of *her* lover). Pierre rises from his wheelchair. He is no longer a cripple, he can speak, he pours a drink. 'Let's take a vacation, go to the mountains.' 'Do you hear?' she replies, and looking out of her Paris window we see the open landau in the country landscape. The coachmen from the opening scene are driving it down the country lane, towards Pierre and Séverine. It has come to take them to the château?

This summary does even less than skeletal justice to the complex enchantments of *Belle de Jour*. Before moving on to a discussion of the reaction it provoked, here, at random, is a brief of particulars which after three viewings of the film stand out strongly:

— Geneviève Page as Madame Anaïs: one of the great performances of the screen in recent years; and most uncanny it is, since the role, as written, is rather one-dimensional.

— None of the film's 'fantasies' are in the book — the girl refusing the host is of course plumb Buñuel. He discards, however, a ferociously Buñuelian item which occurs at the beginning of Kessel's novel. During the last days at winter sports, Séverine falls ill; by the time she returns to her Paris home, a near-fatal case of pneumonia has developed. And it is at *this* point that she begins to be aware of her disquieting sensuality, after the doctors 'have delivered her body to the bites of leeches.'

— When the bonbon magnate (Francis Blanche) invites the girls at the house to drink a bottle of champagne with him, the sequence is so superbly articulated, although unostentatiously edited, that its climax, as the cork pops (a miraculously 'right' placed high-angle group shot), physically imposes itself as a major moment in the film, even though the scene itself is of relatively little importance. There is no precedent in Buñuel's work for such a purely formal 'state of grace'.

— It is early in the film. Séverine returns home, after the disturbing taxi ride during which brothels were discussed. Flowers are brought in, sent by Husson. She drops the vase. 'What's the matter with me today?' she mutters. Until this point, colour in the film has been cool and non-committal. Now, the visual shock of the red roses sprawled on the floor is tremendous — out of all proportion to the apparent seriousness of the incident. A chromatic premonition. As if she had opened a tin of sardines and a live cobra had popped out.

A few years ago, when another masterpiece, Dreyer's *Gertrud*, had its world première in Paris, kilometres of indignation, abuse, and downright foolishness were spat out into print. History has repeated itself with *Belle de Jour* — right down to *Cahiers du Cinéma* belatedly tipping the scales back to sanity again (*Cahiers* 191, 192) with articles more cogent and perceptive; above all, less concerned with protecting Paris concierges from the mischievous productions of dirty old Danish and Spanish cinéastes.

*Positif*, in its July issue, also counter-attacks with a first page editorial: ' The brilliant brains of our critics manifested in chorus the disappointment caused them by *Belle de Jour* . . . thus proving the softening of their own cortexes. This united front of mediocrities was just the most recent attack on one of Buñuel's best films. The producers had already taken up the censor's shears themselves and adulterated it. In our next number we will run the articles the film deserves, but as of now, we would like to assure all of the above gentlemen of our hearty scorn.'

What had the ' above gentlemen ' said? Here are a few pearls:

Garson in *L'Aurore*: ' The ensemble is indecorous.'

Baroncelli in *Le Monde*: '. . . prosaic . . . mediocrity . . . platitude. . . . One can't believe that such bad dreams could go on inside Catherine Deneuve's pretty head.' [It is precisely because Buñuel knows better than anyone else what *can* go on inside pretty heads that his casting of the part is perfect. Deneuve's glacial in-gazing is a wondrous sight. She often looks as impressively opaque as Ingres' ' La Grande Odalisque '; sometimes like *Marnie* reading between the lines in *Alice in Wonderland*. The more Séverine the *grande bourgeoise* ' degrades ' herself, the more beautiful and blooming the actress becomes. Her finest role.]

Mohrt in *Carrefour* : ' The average moviegoer's disappoint-ment is justified.' [The average moviegoer has made *Belle de Jour* into one of the biggest box-office successes of the year. It has just entered its third month of unbroken first run showings at three of Paris's largest cinemas.]

Marcabru in *Arts*: 'A radical-socialist film . . . short of breath and heart. . . . The director has benefited from a sympathy from the critics so excessive that it's close to blind-ness. . . . Buñuel has fallen on his face two times out of three for many years. He has been given the benefit of the doubt because of his age . . . he shouldn't take advantage of it.'

Henry Chapier in *Combat*: 'Buñuel has lost Kessel's generous sentimentality, the marvellous way Kessel knows how to make vice sympathetic.' [Buñuel needs sentimentality like Titian needed colour-blindness. He has never been concerned with vice as such — he may not even know what it is. If he has read Chapier, he may know now : pushing sentimentality is vice.]

M. Chapier again : ' Upper middle-class Parisian women are no longer restrained by sexual taboos, and we could only believe such a story if it were taking place in Spain . . . or at most in Bordeaux or Rouen.' [Is French Puritanism such a thing of the past? Far from it. It is merely something foreign tourists, their eyes filled with postcard visions of Pigalle *filles de joie*, can't be expected to know about, and something most Frenchmen, *their* eyes filled with Fifth Republic State TV homilies, prefer to ignore. It was, after all, only a few weeks ago — in 1967 — that a French law dating from 1922, making it a criminal offence to disseminate any information in favour of birth control, was finally abrogated. It was under the current Gaullist régime, and while the far side of the moon was being photographed, that the hoary works of Havelock Ellis were banned in France. If all the excellent books outlawed under ' Aunt Yvonne's ' reign of public morality were put on shelves, they would constitute a rich modern library. Where does M. Chapier find his unrestrained upper-class Parisian women? He may have been seeing too many old Lubitsch films laid in Paris.]

All of the boys had a really hard time finding their way out of the last reel. Georges Sadoul is an old friend of the director, and don't get him wrong, he does *like* the film, but it's certainly a good thing ' Buñuel put a lot of humour in it . . . otherwise certain sequences would be nauseating.' Sadoul thinks that Séverine's husband just gets well at the end. Aubriant in *Candide* tells us that Pierre was only pretending to be wounded — in a dream. And Marcel Martin, in *Cinéma 67*, strains at an imaginary gnat and swallows ten camels. For him much of the film is dream, but since Buñuel is satirising bourgeois characters, the dialogue is banal on purpose and the colour is mediocre (in truth Sacha Vierny's autumnal Eastmancolor camerawork is superb), because naughty Séverine must have been looking at some faded old blue films before the story started. This ' coloured ' her thoughts!

Only one strong sensible voice has so far been heard in this wilderness of obfuscation : Jean-André Fieschi, in a refreshingly sane piece in *Cahiers* which presents a well-reasoned argument against ' a unilateral reading of the film.'

Indeed, it is impossible and unnecessary to decide whether the end of *Belle de Jour* conveys a shift from fantasy to reality or vice versa. The ambiguity is as immanent in the film, as deliberately Buñuel's, as the tranquil nobility of his point of view — a decent neutrality which condemns no one. He does not side with Séverine, nor can he regard her as a pervert. She has her reasons; but so does everyone else. Neither he nor his heroine wastes a minute worrying about Divine punishment. In accepting herself, Séverine liberates herself. She is no longer *une grande bourgeoise*, but a human being who has undergone a shattering *and* enchanting apprenticeship. But instead of a Hollywood-style clinch at fadeout time, we and she can content ourselves with visions of Séverine, joyful handmaiden at her husband's wheelchair-side *and* (or) riding with Pierre in the magic lantern of her mind down a beautiful country lane, where at any moment he may stop the carriage and deal her the merely divinely human punishment which to her is another name for love.

ELLIOT STEIN
1967

# BELLE DE JOUR

Luis Buñuel's *Belle de Jour* has evoked in many critiques that all-purpose adjective 'beautiful.' Catherine Deneuve is undeniably beautiful, never more so than in this context of Buñuelian perversity, and almost any meaningfully designed colour film seems beautiful if only because the vast subconscious sea of the cinema is safely gelatinized within the frames of an academic painting. Describing a film as beautiful is unfortunately too often a device to end discussion, particularly nowadays when irrationality and hysteria have become institutionalized as life styles. *Elvira Madigan* is beautiful in the way flowery poems are poetical, not through functional expressiveness but through lyrical excessiveness. *Bonnie and Clyde* is beautiful when its luminously lyrical close-ups involve the audience with the killers, but the film is equally beautiful when its concluding slow-motion ballet of death and transfiguration takes the audience off the hook by distancing the characters back into legend and fantasy. The fact that the close-ups contradict the distancing is immaterial to the film's admirers. *Bonnie and Clyde* is beautiful, and consistency is the hobgoblin of little minds.

I would argue that *Belle de Jour* is indeed a beautiful film, but not because of any anaesthetizing aesthetic of benevolently mindless lyricism. Nor is the film beautiful because its director's visual style transcends its sordid subject. The beauty of *Belle de Jour* is the beauty of artistic rigour and adaptable intelligence. Given what Buñuel is at sixty-seven and what he has done in forty years and twenty-seven projects of film-making and what and whom he had to work with and for, *Belle de Jour* reverberates with the cruel logic of formal necessity. From the opening shot of an open carriage approaching the camera at an oblique ground-level angle to the closing shot of an open carriage passing the camera at an oblique overhead angle, the film progresses inexorably upward, an ascent of assent, from the reverie of suppressed desires to the revela-

21

tion of fulfilled fantasies. But whose desires and whose fantasies? Buñuel's? His heroine's? Actually a bit of both. The exact proportion of subjective contemplation to objective correlative can best be calculated by comparing Joseph Kessel's basic anecdotal material with what appears on the screen.

In his preface to *Belle de Jour*, Kessel writes: ' The subject of *Belle de Jour* is not Séverine's sensual aberration; it is her love for Pierre independent of that aberration, and it is the tragedy of that love.' Kessel concludes his preface with a reprovingly rhetorical question for those critics who dismissed *Belle de Jour* as a piece of pathological observation : ' Shall I be the only one to pity Séverine, and to love her? '

The ' sensual aberration ' of which Kessel writes undoubtedly seemed more shocking in 1929, when the first French edition was published, than it would seem in the current period of erotic escalation. Séverine Sérizy, happily married to a handsome young surgeon, goes to work in a house of ill-repute, actually less a house than an intimate apartment. The money involved is less the motivation than the pretext for her action. Pierre, her husband, provides for her material needs handsomely, but his respectfully temporizing caresses fail to satisfy her psychic need for brutal degradation, a need first awakened by a malodorous molester when she was a child of eight. To preserve a façade of marital respectability, Séverine works at her obsessive profession only afternoons from two to five, the mystery of her matinée schedule causing her to be christened Belle de Jour. Kessel's novel, like his heroine, is fatally divided between clinical observations on sexual psychology and novelistic contrivances to overcome the innate lethargy of a woman of leisure. Husson, a weary sensualist in her husband's circle of friends, is a particularly intricate contrivance in that he triggers much of the novel's intrigue. It is Husson who first alerts Séverine to her own frustrations by his unwelcome advances. It is he who inadvertently supplies her with the address of her sensual destiny, and who, discovering her double life, poses such a threat to her non-Belle-de-Jour existence that he precipitates, almost innocently, the final catastrophe.

Marcel, a gold-toothed gangster infatuated with Belle de Jour, provides a violently melodramatic climax to the novel, by agreeing to murder Husson to preserve Séverine's secret and Belle de Jour's respect. Irony is piled upon irony as Marcel's assault on Husson is deflected by Pierre, who is so grievously wounded that he is confined for life to helpless paralysis in a wheelchair. Marcel and Husson remain silent about Belle de Jour, thus enabling Séverine to escape a public scandal and even prosecution, but, perverse to the end, she confesses everything to Pierre, and is rewarded not with his forgiveness but with stern silence.

Buñuel and his co-scenarist Jean-Claude Carrière retained most of the characters of the novel. Séverine goes to work for Madame Anaïs in both novel and film, and Belle de Jour's colleagues are Charlotte and Mathilde in both versions. The most striking variation between novel and film is in the elaborately structured dream apparatus of the film. Kessel's Séverine never dreams the concrete images of Buñuel's surreal reveries of feminine masochism. There are no floggings in the book as there are in the film, no binding of hands with ropes, no sealing of mouths, no splattering with mud. Kessel's Séverine never really dreams at all; she merely recollects the past and anticipates the future. If the novel had been filmed in the thirties or the forties by a French director trained in the Tradition of Quality, a Marcel Carné or Claude Autant-Lara perhaps, Séverine would probably have been played with many shimmering close-ups to dramatize the desperate conflict between her feelings and her senses. The background music would have been exquisitely sentimental. Except for the bells that signal the movement of the horse-drawn carriage, Buñuel uses no music whatsoever. No Simon and Garfunkel, no Beatles, no Donovan, not even the realistically based music of radios and record players. There is no radio or television in the modern world of Belle de Jour, but there is a Geisha Club credit card. Buñuel has stripped modernity of its specificity. Thus we are not bothered so much by the suspicion that horse-drawn carriages are not as likely to figure in the reveries of Séverine's (or Catherine Deneuve's) generation as in the memories of Buñuel's. The fact that Buñuel does not employ music in *Belle de Jour* is not significant as a matter of general aesthetic policy. Buñuel himself has derived ironic counterpoint from the musical backgrounds of such recent films as *Viridiana* and *Simon of the Desert*. He must have felt that he didn't need music to underscore the fundamental irony implicit in a woman with the face of an angel and the lusts of a devil. Still, *Belle de Jour* overcomes an awesome handicap of affect by disdaining the facile frissons of music.

Many of the script changes were dictated by the differences in the media. Pierre emerges through Jean Sorel as a much duller character than in the book, but it is difficult to see what any director can do with the character of the Noble Husband in such a grotesque context. The changes in Husson's character are more meaningful. Kessel's Husson was more mannered in his ennui, but he takes advantage of Séverine's degraded status as Belle de Jour to possess her body. Buñuel's Husson (Michel Piccoli) is more fastidious; he loses interest in Séverine at precisely the instant she becomes available to him as Belle de Jour. But it is Buñuel's Husson who tells Pierre of Belle de Jour after the accident; Kessel's Husson never seriously contemplated such a course of action before or after.

Kessel wants us to love Séverine by identifying with her; Buñuel wants us to understand Séverine by contemplating the nature of her obsession. Instead of indulging in Kessel's sentimental psychology by staring into Catherine Deneuve's eyes, Buñuel fragments Deneuve's body into its erotic constituents. His shots of feet, hands, legs, shoes, stockings, undergarments, etc., are the shots not only of a fetishist, but of a cubist, a director concerned simultaneously with the parts and their effect on the whole. Buñuel's graceful camera movements convey Deneuve to her sensual destiny through her black patent-leather shoes, and to her final reverie through her ringed fingers feeling their way along the furniture with the tactile tenderness of a mystical sensuality, Séverine's, Deneuve's or Buñuel's, it makes little difference.

The beauty of the filmed version of *Belle de Jour* arises from its implication of Buñuel in its vision of the world. It is Buñuel himself who is the most devoted patron of *chez* Madame Anaïs, and the most pathetic admirer of Catherine Deneuve's Séverine-Belle de Jour. Never before has Buñuel's view of the spectacle seemed so obliquely Ophulsian in its

24

shy gaze from behind curtains, windows, and even peepholes. Buñuel's love of Séverine is greater than Kessel's, simply because Buñuel sees Belle de Jour as Séverine's liberator. The sensuality of *Belle de Jour* is not metaphorical like Genêt's in *The Balcony* or Albee's in *Everything in the Garden*. Most writers, even the most radical, treat prostitution as a symptom of a social malaise and not as a concrete manifestation of a universal impulse. Buñuel reminds us once again in *Belle de Jour* that he is one of the few men of the left not afflicted by puritanism and bourgeois notions of chastity and fidelity. The difference between Buñuel and, say, Genêt is not entirely a difference between a man of images and a man of words. What distinguishes *Belle de Jour* from most movies is the impression it gives of having been seen in its director's mind long before it was shot. There is a preconceived exactness to its images that will inevitably disconcert middlebrow film critics, especially those who are highbrows in other cultural sectors. It is only the specialist in film who can fully appreciate the directness of Buñuel's image above and beyond the novelistic nuances he sacrifices on the altars of shock and laughter.

The ending of *Belle de Jour* is tantalizingly open as narrative. Husson has told Pierre about Belle de Jour, or at least we presume so. Buñuel does not show the scene, and we are not obliged to believe anything we do not see, but there is no particular reason to believe that Husson has not carried out his stated intention. Buñuel does not cast his audience adrift in a sea of ambiguity at every opportunity; he is simply not that interested in dramatic suspense. Séverine enters Pierre's room, and for the first time in the film Buñuel's technique obscures the flow of action. Buñuel breaks up the spatial unity of the scene with alternative sights and sounds to indicate a range of possibilities. Cut to Jean Sorel's tear-stained face. Pierre Knows All and Feels Betrayed. Cut to his crumpled upturned hand. Pierre is Dead from the Shock of His Grief. Cut on the sound track to the bells of a carriage, and to Sorel's voice asking of Deneuve's pensive face what Séverine is thinking. Everything Turns Back to Fantasy.

Or does it? Some critics have suggested that Séverine has been cured of her masochistic obsession by becoming Belle de

Jour. Hence the empty carriage at the end of the film. She will no longer take *that* trip. One French critic has argued that the entire film is a dream, but the big problem with such an argument is Buñuel's visually explicit brand of surrealism. Earlier in the film, Husson calls on Séverine at her home and is rudely rebuffed. Buñuel cuts immediately to a shockingly 'cute' Boy-Girl-profile two-shot of Séverine and Husson at the ski lodge. As the camera pulls back, we see Jean Sorel and Macha Meril at the same table. It must be a dream, we assure ourselves, while Séverine and Husson slip out of sight under the table to perform some unspeakable act of sacrilege against bourgeois society. The table begins to bump up and down, but the deserted partners, Sorel and Meril, are only mildly concerned. Buñuel has transported *Belle de Jour* back to *L'Age d'Or*, but the effect of the scene is unsettling if we accept it as occurring in Séverine's mind. Here I think Buñuel slipped into a sadistic attitude of his own toward Pierre, since this is the only scene in the film in which Pierre is made to look completely ridiculous. The key to the scene, however, is not Séverine's characterization but Buñuel's satiric attitude toward Hollywood sentimentality. The profile shot more than the table-bumping gives the show away, but audiences would never 'get' the joke without the table-bumping, and Buñuel does not disdain vulgarity as one of the strategies of surrealism.

Actually we are such Puritans that we talk of surrealism almost exclusively in the solemn terms of social defiance. Humour is only a means to an end, but not an end in itself. No, never? Well, hardly ever. And in Buñuel's case laughter serves to disinfect libertinism of its satanic aura. If we can laugh at the prissiness of perversion and the fastidiousness of fetishism, not with smug superiority, but with carnal complicity, we become too implicated to remain indifferent. Buñuel's masochist, unlike Genêt's in *The Balcony*, satisfies his devious lechery by stroking the thighs of his professionally cruel mistress. Buñuel's brothel is a brothel and not one of Genêt's microcosms, and Buñuel's sensuality turns in upon itself as an enclosed experience devoid of allegorical significance.

Similarly, the entire film turns in upon itself by ending with the same question with which it began: 'Séverine, what are you thinking about?' And Séverine tells the truth in her fashion. She thinks of places and conveyances and trips and herds of Spanish bulls named Remorse except one named Expiation. At the end, she is still dreaming, and who is to say that the dream is any less real or vivid than the reality it accompanies? Certainly not Buñuel's probing but compassionate camera. There are several possible interpretations of Buñuel's ending, but the formal symmetry of the film makes the debate academic. Buñuel is ultimately ambiguous so as not to moralize about his subject. He wishes neither to punish Séverine nor to reward her. He prefers to contemplate the grace with which she accepts her fate, and Buñuel is nothing if not fatalistic. Even the hapless husband is granted a mystical premonition when he sees an empty wheelchair in the street. It is destined for him, and the concreteness of Buñuel's visual imagery is so intense that we feel that the wheelchair is destined for Pierre as Pierre is destined for the wheelchair.

Buñuel's fatalism actually undercuts the suspense of the narrative to the extent that there is no intellectual pressure for a resolved ending. Between the fatalism and the formal symmetry, *Belle de Jour* seems completely articulated as a Buñuelian statement. We do not have to know what we are not meant to know, and Buñuel establishes a precedent within his film for the ambiguity of his ending. This precedent involves Madame Anaïs, after Séverine the most absorbing character in the film. Alone of all the characters, Madame Anaïs is the truth-seeker, and she is inevitably far from the mark. She misunderstands the motivations of Belle de Jour from the outset, and she misinterprets Belle de Jour's departure. Still, she is always staring at Belle de Jour as if it were possible to peel away layers of lacquered flesh to the raw impulses underneath. The scenes in which Geneviève Page's Madame Anaïs gazes with loving curiosity at Catherine Deneuve's Belle de Jour gleam with a psychological insight not customary with Buñuel, or, as rigorously empirical aestheticians would have it, the scenes gleam with the appearance of a psychological insight, the very beautiful appearance derived from two extraordinary screen incarnations.

The great irony of *Belle de Jour* is that a sixty-seven-year-old Spanish surrealist has set out to liberate humanity of its bourgeois sentimentality only to collide with the most sentimental generation of flowery feelings in human history.

ANDREW SARRIS

CREDITS:

| | |
|---|---|
| Scenario by | Luis Buñuel |
| Based on the novel by | Joseph Kessel of the Académie Française |
| Directed by | Luis Buñuel |
| Produced by | Robert and Raymond Hakim |
| Production companies | Paris Film Production (Paris) Five Film (Rome) |
| Director of photography | Sacha Vierney |
| Chief cameraman | Philippe Brun |
| Assistant cameramen | Pierre Li, Lionel Legros |
| Art director | Robert Clavel |
| Assistant art director | Marc Robert Desages |
| First assistant director | Pierre Lary |
| Second assistant director | Jacques Fraenkl |
| Production director | Henri Baum |
| Production manager | Robert Demollière |
| Edited by | Louisette Hautecoeur |
| Assistant editor | Walter Spohr |
| Sound engineer | René Longuet |
| Sound assistant | Pierre Davoust |
| Set designer | Maurice Barnathan |
| Unit manager | Marc Goldstaub |
| Continuity girl | Suzanne Durrenberger |
| Production secretary | Jacqueline Delhomme |
| Stills photographer | Raymond Voinquel |
| Props | Pierre Roudeix |
| Wardrobe | Hélène Nourry |
| Catherine Deneuve's wardrobe | Yves Saint Laurent |
| Make-up | Janine Jarreau |
| Coiffure | Simone Knapp |
| Interior scenes | Franstudio (Saint-Maurice) |
| Process | Eastmancolor |
| Length | 8910 feet |
| Running time | 100 minutes |
| Laboratory | GTC Joinville |
| Sound recording studio | Poste Parisien |

29

CAST :

| | |
|---|---|
| Séverine | Catherine Deneuve |
| Pierre | Jean Sorel |
| Husson | Michel Piccoli |
| Anaïs | Geneviève Page |
| Hippolyte | Francisco Rabal |
| Marcel | Pierre Clementi |
| Charlotte | Françoise Fabian |
| Mathilde | Maria Latour |
| M. Adolphe | Francis Blanche |
| The Duke | Georges Marchal |
| The Professor | François Maistre |
| Renée | Macha Meril |
| Pallas | Muni |
| Catherine | Dominique Dandrieux |
| Thin-faced man | Bernard Fresson |
| Séverine as a child | Brigitte Parmentier |
| with | Claude Cerval |
| | Michel Charrel |
| | Iska Khan |
| | Marcel Charvey |

# BELLE DE JOUR

*Introductory Note*

In this film we have attempted to bring out the masochistic nature of Séverine's impulses. To achieve this, her story is interrupted a number of times by sequences which are either childhood memories or, more often, daydreams, in which certain typical obsessions appear and reappear.

Although these sequences are intended to be imaginary, no distinction, either in the picture or in the sound, is made between them and the other sequences of the film, which seem to describe objectively the relationships between the principal characters and the development of these relationships.

*[The scene is a smart café, situated in an elegant neighbourhood in the west of Paris, not far from the Bois de Boulogne. A number of tables on the terrace are occupied. SEVERINE is sitting alone, seemingly at a loose end. She pays her bill and seems to be waiting for someone. After a while, she looks towards the street and gives an involuntary start of surprise.

An open landau has just come to a stop at the kerb in front of the café. The landau is pulled by two horses. A COACHMAN and a FOOTMAN, both in livery, are sitting very stiffly on the front seat. PIERRE, SEVERINE's husband, gets down from the landau with a smile and waves to his wife.

SEVERINE reacts cautiously. She gets up and goes towards her husband, surprised to see him in such an equipage. PIERRE takes her in his arms and kisses her, saying at the same time:

PIERRE : *Happy birthday* . . .

SEVERINE points to the landau and asks:

_____

\* The whole of this initial sequence in square brackets is taken from Buñuel's original script and does not appear in the film.

SEVERINE : *What's that?*

PIERRE smiling simply : *My first present* . . . He turns towards the landau and adds : *Do you like it?*

SEVERINE taken aback : *What a strange idea* . . .

PIERRE : *I've often heard you say that your dream would be to go out in a landau* . . . *So, there you are* . . .

SEVERINE shakes her head and says reasonably :

SEVERINE : *Pierre, you're mad* . . . *I might have said that, but* . . .

PIERRE pointing to the step : *Well, are you getting in?*

SEVERINE : *Of course!*

A couple, obviously getting on in years, are seated at a neighbouring table on the terrace. Looking at the landau with a certain contempt, the man says :

CUSTOMER : *Anyway, I prefer my fifteen hundred.*

Turning her attention again to the pastry she is eating, his wife remarks with obvious bitterness :

CUSTOMER'S WIFE : *They're just showing off, that's all.*

SEVERINE has got into the landau first. She looks around her and tries the seats for comfort. PIERRE seats himself near her and says :

PIERRE : *The seats are a bit hard, but the suspension is very soft* . . .

SEVERINE breathing in : *And it smells of leather* . . .

Her look is then attracted by the COACHMAN and the FOOTMAN, whose backs, stiff and unmoving, are turned towards them. They both have impressively broad shoulders. Leaning towards PIERRE, and making a slight gesture towards the two men, SEVERINE asks in a low voice :

SEVERINE : *Where did you find those two thugs?*

PIERRE placing a finger to his lips : *Shhh* . . .

The two men have heard that they are being talked about. They are both enormous. Their faces look as though they have been carved out with an axe; their expression is bestial, their smile sinister. The COACHMAN looks as though he hasn't shaved for three days. PIERRE gives them the order to move off :

PIERRE off : *To the woods, now!*

The horses move off at a trot. The bells which are attached

to the horses' harness can be heard ringing.

Leaving behind the last buildings of Paris, the landau enters the Bois de Boulogne amid a stream of cars which overtake it and pass it in the opposite direction.

Inside the landau, SEVERINE has got over her first feeling of surprise and is now looking around her indifferently, even sullenly, as if already bored. PIERRE has put his arm round his wife's shoulders.

The landau leaves the main avenue and goes off along a secondary avenue in the Bois de Boulogne. There are far fewer cars.]

The credits come up against a long shot of a secluded track in the Bois de Boulogne; it is autumn. The open landau drawn by two horses, with the liveried COACHMAN and FOOTMAN, comes towards camera with a jingle of harness. As it draws near we see PIERRE seated in the landau with his arm round his wife, SEVERINE. The jingle of harness grows louder and there are sounds of cars hooting in the distance. Camera pans slowly left with the landau as it moves past and away down an avenue towards the river, then tilts up to show the treetops above. Everything is peaceful and pleasant.

Long shot of the landau coming down another deserted avenue towards camera, which tracks in towards it. The jingle of harness continues.

Low angle close-up tracking out in front of the two horses, the COACHMAN and FOOTMAN sitting on the box behind. (Still on page 65)

Medium close-up of PIERRE and SEVERINE in the back of the moving landau. PIERRE leans towards SEVERINE and asks her:

PIERRE : *Would you like me to tell you a secret, Séverine?*

She looks at him and nods her head without replying.

PIERRE taking her hand : *I love you more every day . . .*

SEVERINE with a fleeting smile : *So do I, Pierre . . . I've only got you in the whole world, but . . .*

She stops, a little ashamed.

PIERRE : *But what? . . .*

She does not reply. PIERRE looks down at SEVERINE's

34

hand in his; he carries on, tenderly and gently:

PIERRE after a pause: *So would I like everything to be perfect
. . . For your coldness to go . . .* He leans forward and tries
to kiss her.

These remarks seem to put SEVERINE in a bad temper.
Irritated, she turns away and replies sharply to PIERRE.

SEVERINE: *Don't say any more about that, please.* She jerks
her hand from his.

PIERRE: *I didn't want to annoy you . . . You know that the
only thing I feel towards you is tenderness . . .*

SEVERINE, staring vaguely ahead, says somewhat bitterly:

SEVERINE: *What good is your tenderness to me?*

PIERRE draws away. He looks pained. He glances across
at the side of the track and says:

PIERRE: *You can be really cruel to me when you feel like
it . . .*

SEVERINE lowering her eyes: *I'm sorry, Pierre . . .*

Close-up of PIERRE, looking at the trees and bushes
which they are passing on either side of the track. His
gaze becomes fixed on a certain spot. He seems to be
very interested in something.

Tracking shot of what he sees. About twenty yards from
the track there is a fine tree, standing alone in the middle
of a clearing which is surrounded by dense thickets. The
landau moves past the clearing; then, in a cold, firm
tone, PIERRE gives an order to the COACHMAN.

PIERRE off, to the COACHMAN: *Stop!* The carriage slows down.

Medium shot: the carriage stops. (Still on page 65) The
expression on PIERRE's face has completely changed. He
has lost all his gentleness and softness. There is a new
light in his eye and his mouth is set. He gets out and, in
an entirely different voice, brusque and authoritarian, he
says to his wife:

PIERRE to SEVERINE: *Get down.*

SEVERINE, not moving, looks at him uncomprehendingly.
She looks extremely surprised by the change in PIERRE's
behaviour.

SEVERINE: *Why? What's got into you?*

PIERRE louder: *I told you to get down!*

35

SEVERINE : *Why?*

He seizes her by the wrist and pulls her violently towards him, as though he wanted to drag her from the carriage.

PIERRE : *Come on!*

SEVERINE resists with all her strength and cries out, suddenly afraid :

SEVERINE : *Leave me alone!*

PIERRE pulling harder : *Come on!*

SEVERINE : *Leave me alone!*

PIERRE violently : *Come on!*

SEVERINE almost screaming : *Leave me alone!*

PIERRE lets her go and turns to the COACHMAN and FOOTMAN. Camera pans right, tilting up towards them and cutting out PIERRE as he addresses them brusquely :

PIERRE off : *Do what I told you to.*

They turn round. Camera tilts down and pans back again as the two men get down from their seat and come towards SEVERINE. She watches them approaching her with the greatest terror. In spite of her cries and her efforts at resistance, PIERRE and the FOOTMAN seize SEVERINE roughly and force her to descend.

SEVERINE crying out : *How dare you? . . . Let me go, you brutes! Let me go!*

PIERRE moves away, leaving her struggling, held by the COACHMAN and FOOTMAN. They come forward.

Medium close-up tracking with the two men as they haul SEVERINE struggling through the undergrowth.

SEVERINE desperately : *It's not my fault. I was going to explain everything!*

PIERRE brutally, off-screen : *Get a move on. There's no need to be afraid of hurting her, the little tart! Hurry up!* He moves past them.

SEVERINE gasping : *It's your fault too, Pierre. I can explain everything.*

COACHMAN letting go of her as they pass a tree : *Shut up, madame, or I'll smash your face in!*

Camera pans slightly right to include PIERRE, who stands watching a little way ahead, holding a coil of rope which he has taken from the boot of the landau. With a brutal shove in the back, the FOOTMAN sends SEVERINE rolling on the ground.

High angle medium close-up of SEVERINE's legs and red skirt. Camera tracks with her as she is dragged along the ground and tilts up to include the two servants, who are dragging her towards the clearing.

SEVERINE : *Stop, please stop! Tell them to let me go!*

Medium close-up, tracking left with PIERRE. He moves across the frame, followed by SEVERINE, who is now walking along, gagged and held from behind by the two servants. SEVERINE stumbles, rips the gag from her mouth and shouts desperately :

SEVERINE : *Help!*

Camera tracks in and halts. PIERRE rushes back and brutally pushes the gag back over her mouth. (Still on page 65)

PIERRE : *Shut up, slut!*

The COACHMAN tightens the gag as PIERRE goes off again.

PIERRE off : *Come on!*

Camera pans left, including PIERRE again, and tracks after them as they move on.

SEVERINE is now at the foot of the tree. High angle close-up of her hands as PIERRE ties them with the rope.

Medium shot of the two of them. Behind them, the COACHMAN stands holding the other end of the rope, which is slung over a branch. PIERRE addresses him curtly.

PIERRE : *Pull!*

The COACHMAN does so, raising SEVERINE's arms in the air, then goes behind the tree trunk to make the rope fast. SEVERINE has stopped struggling and is turned towards the tree. PIERRE comes round behind her, takes the gag out of her mouth and says in a very threatening, fierce tone :

PIERRE : *Don't scream. If you scream, I'll kill you, you understand?*

He begins to rip his wife's clothes — first the upper part of her dress, then her brassière, leaving her back and shoulders naked.

37

SEVERINE desperately : *Pierre, Pierre, I beg of you* . . . *I beg your forgiveness, Pierre, with all my heart* . . . (Still on page 65)

PIERRE moves back a few paces and the two servants appear in back view in the foreground. Each of them has a heavy coachman's whip in his hand. PIERRE walks off between them as they raise their whips.

Low angle medium shot of the COACHMAN and the FOOT-MAN as they begin to take turns in lashing the naked back and shoulders of SEVERINE. We hear the crack of their whips, and SEVERINE's gasps of pain, off.

Very low angle close-up of SEVERINE hanging from the rope as the whips strike her bare shoulders. She cries out :

SEVERINE : *Pierre! Pierre, I beg of you, don't let the cats loose!*

Medium close-up of PIERRE, beneath the overhanging branches of the tree. He lights a cigarette and turns impassively to watch.

Low angle close-up of the COACHMAN delivering his blows with relish.

Medium close-up of SEVERINE, in profile, gasping with pain under the lashes.

Back to the COACHMAN as he continues to whip her.

Back to SEVERINE. The next lash catches her on the arm. She throws her head back and whimpers with pain.

Medium close-up of PIERRE watching, the cigarette hanging from his lips. Camera pans right as he goes up to the FOOTMAN and takes his whip from him.

PIERRE : *All right, that's enough.*

The FOOTMAN stands with his head thrown back. He is out of breath and a slight perspiration can be seen on his forehead.

PIERRE : *She's yours now.* He looks towards SEVERINE, off-screen. *Carry on!* He goes off.

SEVERINE simultaneously, off : *Pierre, I love you.* Silence. Out of breath, she whimpers : *Pierre! Pierre!*

The FOOTMAN hurriedly removes his jacket and hat and throws them on the ground. From the way in which he looks at SEVERINE, it is not difficult to guess his intentions.

38

Low angle medium close-up of the COACHMAN as he stands watching, holding his whip, with an expression of salacious relish on his face.

Medium close-up of SEVERINE, her hands still hanging from the rope. The FOOTMAN comes up behind her and, still wearing his white gloves, lays his hands on her bare shoulders.

Low angle close-up of SEVERINE. There is a mixture of repugnance and pleasure in her look. She is afraid, but at the same time she expects something from this man whose lips are going to touch her in a second. The COACHMAN kisses her in the small of the back and she throws her head back, eyes closed. (Still on page 65) PIERRE is heard off; his tone has completely changed and is quite natural again :

PIERRE off : *What are you thinking about, Séverine?*

Medium close-up of PIERRE, back to camera, in their apartment in Paris. He is standing in front of the bathroom mirror, preparing to go to bed. Camera is looking through the open doorway of the bedroom, and the reflection in the mirror shows PIERRE's face with SEVERINE lying in bed in the background. PIERRE turns and comes to the doorway of the bedroom as he repeats his question.

PIERRE : *What are you thinking about?*

High angle medium close-up of SEVERINE lying in bed; she is in a nightdress, but she is not yet asleep. Her bedside lamp is lit and her eyes are open. Camera tracks in slightly as she seems to wake up to reality. She turns her head slightly towards her husband and says, hesitantly :

SEVERINE : *I was thinking . . . about you . . . about us . . . We were driving together in a landau.*

Reverse angle medium close-up of PIERRE standing in the doorway. He smiles indulgently across at SEVERINE.

PIERRE : *That landau again?*

He turns out the overhead light and camera pans left with him as he walks across to his own bed, next to SEVERINE's.

SEVERINE turning towards him : *I want to kiss you . . .*

PIERRE leans over and kisses her gently, then starts to arrange the pillow on his bed.

PIERRE : *You'll have to get up early tomorrow.*

SEVERINE : *Why?*

PIERRE sitting down on his bed : *To pack the luggage.* Camera tilts down slightly.

SEVERINE : *Are we going somewhere?*

PIERRE : *Yes.*

SEVERINE : *Where?*

PIERRE : *It's a surprise for our wedding anniversary. Since our happiness is already a year old, and the suns of yesteryear . . .*

SEVERINE : *What about the hospital?*

PIERRE : *I want to forget about it for a few days . . . and think only about you.*

Camera tracks in as he moves across and kisses SEVERINE tenderly.

PIERRE : *Happy?*

SEVERINE stroking his head : *Yes, especially when you're here . . . I would like to be with you every minute of the day . . .* (Still on page 66)

She leans forward and puts her arms round him.

High angle medium close-up. They kiss tenderly and gaze at each other for a moment. Then PIERRE gets up, camera tilting with him then tracking out as he draws aside the bedclothes to get in beside her.

Close-up of the two of them. SEVERINE puts out an arm, fending him off as he leans towards her.

SEVERINE : *No, please . . .*

PIERRE turns away, disappointed.

PIERRE : *Sleep well.* He gets up and kisses her on the forehead. High angle medium shot.

PIERRE : *Good night.*

He turns out the bedside lamp and settles himself restlessly in his own bed.

High angle medium close-up of SEVERINE. She turns her head from side to side.

SEVERINE : *Pierre.*

PIERRE off : *Yes?*

SEVERINE : *Forgive me. You are so kind . . . so understand-*

*ing, but I . . .*

Camera pans across to PIERRE, who says brusquely :

PIERRE : *It's all right, go to sleep.* He turns away from her.


\*[PIERRE and SEVERINE are walking alone on the side of a high mountain which is covered here and there with thinly scattered snow. They are dressed for shooting and are carrying guns. SEVERINE slows down and says to PIERRE :

SEVERINE : *I'm tired . . .*

PIERRE : *Just a little bit further. Come this way.*

He leads her a little farther on. Suddenly he stops, bends down and says in a low voice to his wife, stretching out his hand :

PIERRE : *There . . . Look . . .*

Thirty yards away from them, the head of a white fox appears out of a ditch and looks round in every direction.

PIERRE raises his gun, but SEVERINE stops him and says :

SEVERINE : *No . . . Let me . . .*

PIERRE lets her do as she wants. She raises her gun to her shoulder rather clumsily, aims and fires. The fox's head disappears.

The two of them walk across to the ditch and look down into it. The body of the fox can be seen, motionless and rigid. There is a label attached to one of its paws.

SEVERINE seizes hold of it, picks it up and shouts :

SEVERINE turning towards PIERRE : *You've been making fun of me!*

At that moment, laughter can suddenly be heard not far away from them. SEVERINE looks round.

She sees a peasant seated a few yards away; he is looking at her and laughing. It is he who has been manipulating the fox's body.

SEVERINE does not look very pleased. PIERRE goes towards her, smiling, and says :

PIERRE : *Don't hold it against me. Just look what he's got between his teeth.*

---

\* The following sequence in square brackets appears in the original script, but would seem not to have been shot.

41

She opens the rigid jaws of the fox, between which she
finds a jewel-case containing a jewel. PIERRE adds:

PIERRE : *Happy birthday* . . .

SEVERINE throws herself in his arms and they both start
laughing.]


Long shot of a sunlit street in a winter sports resort, with
shops and bars on either side. People are walking to and
fro carrying skis. Camera tracks out in front of PIERRE
and SEVERINE, casually dressed, as they come towards
us, accompanied by RENEE, a friend of SEVERINE'S.
PIERRE slips on some ice. They all laugh.

SEVERINE : *Are you coming to the party at the Grand Hotel?*

RENEE : *I don't know. Husson's always in bed by sunset.*

PIERRE : *Let him sleep and come with us. They say there'll be
snow tonight.*

SEVERINE takes off her sunglasses.

RENEE : *I'd rather go and see the mesmerizer. They say he
performs miracles.*

PIERRE puts his arm round SEVERINE.

SEVERINE : *Well, I wouldn't let myself be put to sleep.*

PIERRE : *A mesmerizer is not the same thing as a hypnotist,
my dear. He makes the sun rise. Hypnotists plunge you into
darkness.*

RENEE : *Well, I must be off.* They all stop. *See you later.
Goodbye.*

PIERRE and SEVERINE : *Goodbye.*

They go off to the left while RENEE goes off to the right.
Long shot of the interior of a bar in the winter sports
resort, in daylight. The atmosphere is warm, lively and
smoke-ridden. Camera tracks after several people moving
across the bar and stops in front of a couple seated at
a table. The woman is RENEE — elegant and bronzed
and aged about thirty. The man who is with her, HENRI
HUSSON, could be thirty-five to forty. He is an ageing
playboy, very carefully dressed. He gazes after every
woman who passes. Without looking at RENEE, he asks
her :

HUSSON : *What time is it?*

42

RENEE looks at her watch and answers:

RENEE: *Five o'clock.* A pause. *If you're bored with me, I'm not keeping you . . .*

Indifferent and somewhat scornful, HUSSON raises his tea-cup as he says:

HUSSON: *One is never bored in a bar . . . It's not like a church, where you're alone with your soul . . .* He puts down his tea-cup. *I'll tell you something pleasant. I love you.* With a total lack of conviction he takes her hand and kisses it.

RENEE in a bored tone: *Thank you.*

HUSSON: *Scars suit you.*

RENEE removing her hand and looking away: *Oh, you bore me!*

[RENEE looks towards the door and, when she sees PIERRE and SEVERINE come in, she cries out:

RENEE: *Look, the Sérizys.*

She waves them to come to their table.

PIERRE and SEVERINE, who have seen her signal, wave back from some way away. Then, seeing that HUSSON is there, SEVERINE stops, turns round and makes as though to go out again.]*

Medium shot. Camera pans with a couple as they walk past the bar counter and go off into another part of the bar. PIERRE and SEVERINE come in, approach camera and stop.

SEVERINE: *No, don't let's go.* She glances behind them. *She's with Husson . . .*

PIERRE: *Too late, he's seen us. What have you got against him? He's an interesting sort of chap, isn't he?*

SEVERINE hostile: *You think so? Well, I don't like the way he looks at me.*

PIERRE: *Come on.*

He makes SEVERINE go in front of him and guides her towards their friends' table off-screen.

High angle long shot of RENEE and HUSSON at their table. HUSSON rises as PIERRE and SEVERINE approach from the foreground. The two men shake hands, while

---

* This section in square brackets appears in the original script but was not seen in the version screened.

the two women kiss like old friends; then PIERRE shakes hands with RENEE.

RENEE : *Hello, you two.*

SEVERINE : *Hello, Renée, had a good day?*

RENEE : *Not bad.*

The newcomers sit down.

Medium close-up of the group. RENEE and PIERRE are in profile in the foreground, HUSSON and SEVERINE facing camera in the background. HUSSON sits down and says, slightly mockingly :

HUSSON : *I saw you go by earlier, arm-in-arm. You were a pleasure to watch. You looked like a newly married couple.* He smiles at SEVERINE.

SEVERINE rather aggressive : *I suppose we looked a bit ridiculous?*

HUSSON : *Oh, no, it looked very beautiful . . . reassuring. As though it was an everyday thing.* Camera tracks in, cutting out the two women, as he addresses PIERRE. *Yet you, Pierre, you sometimes make me uneasy . . . give me a bad conscience. We're so different. One doesn't really meet many men like you. I mean that.*

PIERRE, a little surprised, replies : *Well . . . thanks . . .*

Low angle medium shot, panning with two elegantly dressed women as they pass through the bar and behind the table where the group are sitting. Camera holds on the group. HUSSON gazes after the women as they go off-screen.

HUSSON sighing, to PIERRE : *My God . . . there goes another lost chance of suffering . . .*

PIERRE surprised, turning to HUSSON : *Why do you say that? Do you know them?*

HUSSON : *No.*

PIERRE rather mockingly : *Is that really all you're interested in?* HUSSON possesses a mixture of sincerity and rather pretentious insolence which makes it impossible to put him out.

HUSSON lighting a cigarette : *Yes. Everything else is useless. Absolutely worthless and a waste of time.*

PIERRE : *One of these days, you ought to tell a specialist about your obsessions.*

Close-up of RENEE.

RENEE : *He's rich and idle: they're his two main illnesses.*

Medium close-up of HUSSON, beside SEVERINE.

HUSSON to RENEE : *That and the chase . . . Apart from that I'm particularly fond of the poor, I mean the working class. I think of them particularly when it snows . . . nothing to keep them warm . . . no hope, nothing.*

HUSSON looks at SEVERINE and says to her in the same lighthearted tone :

HUSSON : *You're very attractive, Séverine.*

SEVERINE looks at him fixedly, and replies, ironically :

SEVERINE : *Your compliments are too subtle for me. So be quiet.*

Camera tracks back to include RENEE and PIERRE.

RENEE : *You're asking him to do the impossible.*

HUSSON continues looking at SEVERINE, apparently unconcerned about PIERRE's presence. Suddenly, changing his tone completely, he gets up and says :

HUSSON : *Well, I'll leave you now. I've been here for three hours and I can feel a migraine coming on.* To PIERRE : *It's not too cold outside?*

PIERRE : *No, no. It's quite mild.*

HUSSON : *I'm going to have a breath of fresh air before it gets dark. See you later, Renée.*

RENEE a little sullen : *See you later.*

PIERRE : *Have a good walk . . .*

HUSSON gets up and walks away; the other three gaze after him.

PIERRE : *I like him. He's amusing.*

SEVERINE : *He's strange.*

RENEE : *Worse than that.*

[Before going through the door of the bar, HUSSON wraps himself up carefully, helped by the waiter in charge of the cloakroom. He muffles himself up completely : overcoat, woollen scarf and a fur hat which he pushes well down on his head.]*

---

* This section appears in the original script but was not seen in the version screened.

45

Low angle medium shot of HUSSON coming down the street outside the bar. Looking very cold, he wraps his scarf round his face, and camera pans to follow him as he goes round a corner and off into the distance. The passers-by, skidding on the icy surface, seem to find the weather fairly mild. (Still on page 66)

[We meet SEVERINE again — today's SEVERINE — with her friend RENEE, in a street in Paris. The two women have just been shopping. They are carrying a number of packages. We see them stop a taxi, and both of them climb in. The taxi moves off.]*

Very high angle long shot, panning with the taxi as it moves along a Paris street. There is a roar of traffic. (Still on page 66)

Shot of the road as seen by the TAXI-DRIVER through the windscreen. We hear SEVERINE and RENEE conversing in the back of the taxi :

SEVERINE : *I haven't asked you how Husson is.*

RENEE sulky : *He's fine.*

SEVERINE : *Are you still seeing him?*

RENEE : *Yes, unfortunately . . . Don't talk to me any more about it.*

[RENEE stays silent for a moment, then she continues :

RENEE sighing : *I don't feel up to things at present. I've had nothing but rotten luck.*

SEVERINE : *It'll pass.]***

Medium close-up of the two women in the back of the moving taxi, with the TAXI-DRIVER in the foreground gazing stolidly at the street ahead. RENEE turns to SEVERINE as if she had suddenly remembered something.

RENEE : *Do you remember Henriette?*

SEVERINE : *Yes, very well . . .*

RENEE : *Apparently . . .*

She lowers her voice so that the TAXI-DRIVER can't hear

---

* This section appears in the original script but was not seen in the version screened.

** This piece of dialogue appears in the original script but was not heard in the version screened.

what she is saying and camera tracks forward, losing him.

RENEE: *Apparently she regularly does a turn as a prostitute . . .*

SEVERINE's reaction is absent-minded, almost indifferent, as if she hadn't heard or understood very well.

SEVERINE: *What?*

RENEE still in a low voice: *Yes, in a brothel . . .* Rather excited: *It's supposed to be quite true! Apparently she goes several times a week!*

SEVERINE shakes her head slightly, thoughtful and rather indifferent, as if she was only half listening.

SEVERINE: *Really . . .*

Then her attention strays; she appears to attach no importance to RENEE's confidences. RENEE, somewhat disappointed that she has not been able to stimulate SEVERINE's interest, and not understanding her indifference, insists:

RENEE: *But isn't it fantastic! Henriette!*

SEVERINE turns towards RENEE, who looks at her, smiling somewhat mockingly.

RENEE: *Of course, I know that that's hardly your world . . .*

SEVERINE says to her, as though trying to excuse herself:

SEVERINE: *No, but . . .*

Close-up of RENEE looking towards SEVERINE.

RENEE interrupting her: *Can you imagine it, Séverine? A woman like you or me . . .* She speaks very quickly in a shocked tone *. . . can you see her going with anybody? . . . Once you're there, of course, there's no choice . . . You've got to take whoever comes, old or young, good-looking or not . . .* She stops with a movement of disgust.

Medium close-up of the two of them seen through the side window of the taxi. While RENEE has been speaking, the expression on SEVERINE's face has changed completely. She has become very attentive, but afterwards seems to share RENEE's revulsion.

RENEE: *Even with a man you like, there are times when it's unpleasant . . .*

SEVERINE: *It must be horrible with strangers.* Forcing herself: *But do they still exist, those places?*

47

Resume on medium close-up of the two of them facing camera, the TAXI-DRIVER'S shoulder in the foreground. RENEE makes a vague gesture and the TAXI-DRIVER decides to interrupt at this moment. Without giving the slightest indication, he has followed attentively the conversation which the two women have been carrying on in lowered voices.

TAXI-DRIVER: *Excuse me, ladies* . . . Camera tracks out to include him as he continues with a knowing smile . . . *but they certainly do exist. I assure you.* (Still on page 66)

A slight pause. The two women look at the driver with a certain amount of surprise, then they exchange a look between themselves. The driver has now got going in his conversation and wants nothing better than to carry on.

TAXI-DRIVER: *They're not up to the pre-war joints, maybe. No more red lights, of course.*

Close-up of SEVERINE. (Still on page 66) She remains thoughtful while the TAXI-DRIVER continues off:

TAXI-DRIVER: *You can take it from me, they're not idle. I could show you a good half-dozen.*

Close-up of the TAXI-DRIVER as seen by the women.

TAXI-DRIVER: *It's part of the job, you see . . . I've been driving a cab for twenty years, and I've seen it all . . .*

Resume on close-up of SEVERINE, who is silent, apparently lost in thought. The TAXI-DRIVER continues off:

TAXI-DRIVER: *I've been attacked twice, but I'm none the worse for it . . .*

He stops at last. A pause. SEVERINE does not move. RENEE suddenly interrupts her train of thought and she jumps.

RENEE off: *Hey, what's the matter with you . . . We're there.*

SEVERINE seems to wake up. She turns to RENEE, then looks away again.

[SEVERINE: *Oh, yes, thank you . . . See you tomorrow . . .* RENEE: *See you tomorrow . . .*]*

---

* This piece of dialogue appears in the original script but was not heard in the version screened.

48

Long shot of the street. The taxi approaches camera, which pans right as it rounds a corner and draws in to the kerb in the foreground. SEVERINE gets out clutching some parcels and waves goodbye to RENEE, who remains in the taxi. The taxi moves off and RENEE gives her a friendly wave through the window. SEVERINE does not reply to this gesture. She is standing on the pavement in front of the apartment house where she lives; it is a middle-class, comfortable-looking block in the 6th or 14th *arrondissement*. The block is situated in a quiet side street; the street itself is fairly short and gives onto a more important street or avenue. RENEE's story and the TAXI-DRIVER's conversation have made a vivid impression on SEVERINE. She remains motionless for a second, her packages in her hand, then she turns round, crosses the road and goes into the apartment house. As she does so, camera tracks out and tilts up to show the façade of the building. General shot of the elegantly furnished drawing room in SEVERINE's and PIERRE's apartment. A vase of red roses is standing on a low table between two mustard-coloured sofas. Camera pans right and a MAID appears from the foreground, followed by SEVERINE.

MAID : *These flowers came for you, madame.*
SEVERINE : *Very good. Who sent them?*
MAID : *Monsieur Husson, madame.* She goes off.

SEVERINE crosses the room, apparently thinking of something else. Camera pans left as she puts her handbag down on one of the sofas and goes over to the vase. She stretches out her hand to take hold of the visiting card of the sender, glances at it and throws it down on the table.

SEVERINE turning to the MAID off-screen : *Why did you put them here?*

She picks them up and camera pans right as she carries the vase across to the MAID, who is standing polishing a glass in the adjoining dining room. SEVERINE slips on the polished floor and drops the vase with a crash.

MAID turning round : *I'll go and get a cloth* . . . She bends down and puts the flowers back in the broken vase. *It doesn't matter* . . . *the water was clean.*

49

SEVERINE walks towards camera and goes off to the right.*
Medium close-up, panning right with SEVERINE as, having
taken off her coat, she enters the bathroom and stands in
front of the mirror. She pushes her hair back and looks
at herself attentively. (Still on page 67) She moves back,
then leans forward again to pick up her hairbrush and
catches a flask of perfume with her arm. Camera tilts
down as the flask falls and shatters on the floor. Then
it tilts up again as SEVERINE sits down, and tracks in
towards her. She leans her elbow on the wash-basin and
says to herself:
SEVERINE : *What's the matter with me today?*
Daydreaming, she hears the voice of her mother calling.
SEVERINE'S MOTHER off : *Séverine, come quickly.***

[Interior shot of a corridor, daytime. The corridor is long
and rather dark, terminating in a bend. A LITTLE GIRL
aged eight runs along it, pursuing a ball which she has
thrown. She goes as far as the end of the corridor, then
she runs back. A woman's voice is heard off, calling:
SEVERINE'S MOTHER off : *Séverine, come here quickly!*
LITTLE GIRL : *I'm coming, Mummy!*
She continues to run after her ball in the corridor.
A PLUMBER comes out of a half-open door which leads
to the bathroom. He has just finished putting his equip-
ment away after carrying out some repairs. He is a man
in his prime, full of vigour, but rather greasy and dirty
and unshaven. He has the same brutal face as the FOOT-
MAN in the first sequence in the Bois de Boulogne. He puts
his tool-box in his bag and comes out into the corridor,
closing behind him the door of the bathroom where he
has been working. At that moment the LITTLE GIRL runs
near him in the corridor.

---

* In Buñuel's original script, this scene is slightly different, and it is not
until Séverine goes into the bathroom that she asks the maid, who is
still in the dining room, who sent the flowers.
** In the original script, this call from Séverine's mother occurs only in
the corridor scene which follows. The original version of this scene, as
shown by the two following sections in square brackets, was reduced
in the film as screened to a single shot.

He grabs hold of her as she runs by and, putting one knee on the floor, he squeezes her in his arms.]

High angle medium close-up of the LITTLE GIRL. At first only her legs are visible and a figure in dirty blue overalls is kneeling on the floor beside her. Camera tilts up to show the PLUMBER holding her in his arms. He leans forward and kisses her. She closes her eyes and holds her breath. (Still on page 67) Her mother shouts again, off :

SEVERINE'S MOTHER : *Well, Séverine, are you coming or not?*

[The PLUMBER suddenly lets the LITTLE GIRL go and gets up. She leans against the wall, her eyes closed. The PLUMBER goes out by a door in the corridor and disappears. The LITTLE GIRL slides to the floor and remains motionless.

SEVERINE'S MOTHER off : *What are you doing on the floor?*

The LITTLE GIRL suddenly opens her eyes and raises her head. Then she gets up as quickly as possible and replies to her mother :

LITTLE GIRL : *I slipped, Mummy. I fell.*

She has spoken these words with lowered eyes, a little confused by her lie. Her face is very pale.]

*General shot of PIERRE's study at night. PIERRE has been seated at his desk in the far corner, working by lamplight. He is going over an article or some lecture notes. As the shot begins he walks across the room to reach for a book from the bookcase next to him. Then he stands by the desk looking at the book. SEVERINE, wearing a pink dressing gown over her pyjamas, is sitting in an armchair about two yards away from PIERRE, beside another lamp in the foreground. She is working on some half-finished embroidery. We feel that PIERRE and SEVERINE meet here every evening and sit in the same places. SEVERINE still seems as preoccupied. She soon stops working and asks PIERRE :

SEVERINE : *Will you be long?*

---

* In the original script, this following scene in Pierre's study does not take place until after Séverine has made her first visit to the street where the brothel is situated.

PIERRE without looking up : *I've nearly finished.*

He sits down at his desk. SEVERINE gets up and goes and sits in another armchair just beside him.

Medium close-up of SEVERINE seated in the chair. A pause. She looks at her husband, then asks him :

SEVERINE : *Can I ask you a stupid question?*

PIERRE : *Go ahead.*

SEVERINE leans forward in her armchair and puts both elbows on the desk. Camera tracks out to include PIERRE sitting opposite her in the foreground.

SEVERINE : *Before I knew you, did you often go to those . . .*

She hesitates, as though she was going to use a coarse word, then she says :

SEVERINE : *. . . houses?*

Very surprised, PIERRE stops writing, looks up, looks at his wife and says :

PIERRE : *Houses . . . No, not very often. Why? Does that interest you?*

To hide her real interest, SEVERINE says with assurance :

SEVERINE : *Everything about you interests me . . .* A pause, then she adds : *It's odd, I thought they'd been suppressed . . .*

PIERRE starts working again, replying at the same time :

PIERRE : *They're under cover now . . .*

SEVERINE : *I can't imagine . . . what it's like . . .*

PIERRE : *Listen, I've got work to do.*

SEVERINE : *Please . . .*

Once again PIERRE stops working, rather surprised by his wife's insistence on this unusual subject. As PIERRE speaks, camera tracks slowly round in a semi-circle, holding on the couple, until their positions are reversed and SEVERINE appears in the foreground. (Still on page 67)

PIERRE : *You go in and you see the women there . . . you choose one of them, and spend half an hour with her . . .*

SEVERINE listens almost intensely; he continues :

PIERRE : *When you get out, you feel depressed for the rest of the day, but it can't be helped . . .* Forcing a smile : '*Semen retentum venenum est . . .*'

SEVERINE straightens up suddenly, and says quietly :

SEVERINE : *Shut up!*

Very surprised by this reaction, PIERRE looks at her.

SEVERINE gets up and continues, but this time louder:

SEVERINE: *Shut up . . . Don't talk about it any more . . . Please . . .* She goes off.

High angle medium close-up of PIERRE sitting at his desk. He leans forward, looking puzzled.

PIERRE: *What's the matter with you?*

Camera tilts up and pans right with him as he abandons his work, gets up and goes towards his wife and takes her tenderly in his arms.

PIERRE: *I've never seen you like this. What's wrong?*

SEVERINE: *Nothing . . . I'm a bit tired . . . on edge . . .*

PIERRE: *Go and rest.*

SEVERINE: *Yes, you're right.* She kisses him. *Good night.*

Camera pans left as she moves away towards the bedroom.

PIERRE starting to follow her: *Do you want me to come with you?*

SEVERINE turning in the doorway: *No, no . . .*

She changes her mind and adds weakly, almost like a child:

SEVERINE: *Yes. I'd like you to stay with me until I go to sleep . . .*

Camera tracks in as PIERRE goes towards her and puts his arm round her.

PIERRE: *Won't you ever grow up?* They go into the bedroom.

The scene changes to a tennis club in the daytime. The club consists of several courts, surrounded by a garden and, at one end, a building which houses a changing room and bar.

[SEVERINE is playing in a mixed doubles match with two men and a woman whom we do not know. We see her miss a ball and immediately leave the court, saying:

SEVERINE: *I'm sorry, but I'm giving up.*

The other players stop, rather surprised.]*

High angle medium shot tracking with SEVERINE as she leaves the court and comes up the steps towards the

---

* This section appears in the original script but was not seen in the version screened.

club house. At the top she runs into RENEE, who is also dressed for tennis.

SEVERINE : *Take my place. I can't hit a thing today.*

RENEE : *Are you leaving?*

SEVERINE : *No, I'll wait for you inside. See you later.*

RENEE goes off to the court. Camera pans left with SEVERINE as she goes into the club house.

Inside the club house, camera follows a young, rather pretty woman as she comes down the stairs and goes across to the glass entrance door, where she meets SEVERINE. It is HENRIETTE.

HENRIETTE with a friendly smile : *Hello . . . How are you?*

Rather surprised, SEVERINE, who has recognized her, says:

SEVERINE : *Fine, thanks.*

HENRIETTE her hand on the door : *We don't see you here very often, these days.*

SEVERINE : *No, that's true.*

HENRIETTE : *See you later.* She goes out of the door.

Camera pans with SEVERINE as she walks into the club house, stops and watches the young woman go away. At that moment, HUSSON'S voice is heard very close to her, making her jump.

HUSSON off : *Ah, the mysterious Henriette . . .*

Camera pans as she turns and walks towards him.

HUSSON smiling and pacing about in front of her : *The woman with two faces, the double life . . . It's very interesting . . . Has Renée told you all about it?* (Still on page 67)

Torn between the repugnance which HUSSON has always inspired in her and the interest which she feels in HENRIETTE'S adventure, SEVERINE asks him, but with apparent indifference :

SEVERINE : *Yes, but . . . why?*

HUSSON : *For money. It's as simple as that. The great majority of women who sell themselves, I'm afraid, do it for money.*

He comes round behind her, and turns to face her.

HUSSON : *I'm glad to see you today.*

SEVERINE turns away from him and sits in an armchair, camera tilting down with her.

SEVERINE : *I can't understand women like that.*

Low angle medium close-up of HUSSON. He leans forward, preening himself and proud to show his knowledge of the subject.

HUSSON : *Oh, you know, it's the oldest profession in the world. Nowadays, it's mostly done by telephone . . . Women operating from houses are rarer, anyway.*

High angle medium close-up of SEVERINE as seen by HUSSON. Trying to hide her confusion and the great interest which she feels as he speaks, SEVERINE fiddles with her watch and replies :

SEVERINE scornfully : *Houses you must know very well . . .*

Resume on HUSSON.

HUSSON : *Yes, I used to go a lot. I like them very much. There's a very special atmosphere about them . . . The women are completely enslaved.*

Camera tracks out to include SEVERINE as HUSSON comes towards her. HUSSON cannot guess that she is fascinated by what she is learning.

HUSSON : *I remember . . . especially around the Opéra . . . Oh yes, at Anaïs's, 11 Cité Jean de Saumur . . . I've got some marvellous memories . . .*

Suddenly he leans towards her and kisses her on the neck. SEVERINE jumps up indignantly, looks at him and says :

SEVERINE : *What's the matter with you? Have you gone crazy?*

Completely unashamed, HUSSON answers, with a casual gesture :

HUSSON : *Oh, nothing. ' Cute compulsions ', as the English say . . . An insignificant little impulse . . .*

SEVERINE looks at him with a certain amount of disgust. HUSSON adds, very coolly :

HUSSON : *Séverine, I must see you one of these days . . . Without your husband, of course . . . I admire Pierre a lot, but I'd prefer him not to be there . . .* He circles round and moves towards her.

Medium close-up of the two of them facing each other in profile. HUSSON has taken her by the arm but she shrugs him off with an angry gesture. SEVERINE looks at him one

55

last time, then camera tracks out as she comes forward while HUSSON goes off in the opposite direction. As she walks, she seems thoughtful and preoccupied.

[Suddenly we see HUSSON again, as we have seen him a few moments ago, saying the same words : ]*

HUSSON'S VOICE over : *Madame Anaïs . . . 11 Cité Jean de Saumur.***

SEVERINE pauses, looking thoughtful.

Low angle medium close-up of a Paris street sign which reads : CITE JEAN DE SAUMUR. Camera pans left, tilting down to show SEVERINE as she comes round a corner and halts, looking up at the sign. She is wearing a military style charcoal grey coat and her hair is tucked inside a cloche hat.

Long shot of the street adjoining the Cité Jean de Saumur. Camera pans right to reveal SEVERINE standing on the corner looking up at the sign. The Cité Jean de Saumur is a vast arrangement of apartment blocks standing on three sides of a square. Camera pans with her as she walks along past the railings at the end of the square. She continues walking without turning round, as if she were afraid or ashamed, then halts about twenty yards farther on, by a barber's shop on the opposite corner. She looks round furtively and camera pans back again as she re-crosses the square towards a dairy next to Number 11.

Medium shot of the façade of the dairy. SEVERINE appears from the left and stands looking in the window as if interested in the things which are displayed there. She turns her head and looks at the building out of the corner of her eye. Then she looks in the other direction.

---

* This shot, which appears in the original script, does not occur in the film, where we merely hear Husson's voice as if ringing in Séverine's ears as she walks along.

** In the original script, the address which Husson gives Séverine is 9b rue Virène, and the script gives this name on the street sign in the following sequence. Also, in the script, Séverine arrives in a taxi and cruises past the doorway of the apartment building before getting out.

[She sees a man come along the pavement and go into the building with a rather shameful air, as if he had an uneasy conscience. He looks around him before going in quickly. SEVERINE turns towards the shop window again. The SHOPKEEPER comes out of the shop at that moment and says, very politely:

SHOPKEEPER : *Do you want something, mademoiselle? Have a look inside.*

SEVERINE : *No, no, thank you . . .*]*

Low angle medium close-up tracking with a young woman — obviously a prostitute — as she swings down the street, a cigarette-end hanging from the corner of her mouth. She halts, takes a last drag, throws away the cigarette-end and walks on again.

Resume on the façade of the dairy with SEVERINE standing back to camera in the foreground. Camera pans with the PROSTITUTE as she passes between SEVERINE and the shop window, looking her up and down as she does so, and walks in through the doorway of the adjoining apartment block, swinging her hips. Camera tilts up to show the number 11 above the doorway.

Medium close-up of SEVERINE looking after her. Camera pans with her as she turns and hurries away across the square.

Long shot of an avenue in a public park with a large mansion in the background. Schoolchildren are rushing about playing, shouting at the tops of their voices. Camera tracks to the right as SEVERINE comes towards us and sits down on a bench in the foreground. A bell chimes in the distance.

Medium close-up of SEVERINE sitting on the bench, her head out of frame. She takes a handkerchief out of her handbag and camera tilts up to her face as she wipes away a tear. Another mansion is seen behind her. Apparently very sad, she looks at her watch, then gets up.**

---

* This episode, which occurs in the script only, is replaced in the film by that of the prostitute entering the building.

** This short sequence in the park does not occur at this point in the original script, but appears at a later stage.

57

Low angle medium close-up of SEVERINE, now wearing dark glasses, in the square of the Cité Jean de Saumur. Camera tracks left with her as she crosses the square to the entrance of Number 11. She hesitates, looks at a plate beside the door, looks round furtively, then presses the buzzer and goes in. Camera tracks in on the nameplate beside the door, which reads: MME ANAIS — FASHIONS.

Once inside, SEVERINE avoids the concierge, ignores the lift and goes up directly by the staircase to look for Madame Anaïs's flat. We see her in high angle medium shot as she comes up the stairs. She seems rather anxious, and the higher she gets, the less confident she becomes. She does not have much idea where she is going. She stops and looks around her, (Still on page 67) and camera zooms in to close-up. A voice is heard chanting in Latin off.

[Inside a church, daytime. It is the day of the first communion and while the choir, accompanied by the organ, sing a canticle for the occasion ('I promised when I was baptized . . .'), several young girls in white dresses get ready to receive the Holy Sacrament. The PRIEST, carrying the ciborium, approaches one of them, whom we recognize as the LITTLE GIRL running in the corridor. She looks very frightened. Her mouth is closed.]*

High angle medium shot of the PRIEST with a red-capped server on either side of him. Camera moves in to medium close-up of his hands as he dips a wafer in the golden chalice, pronouncing the words of the ritual. (Stills on page 68)

PRIEST: '*Corpus domini nostri Jesus Christi custodiat animam tuam in vitam aeternam . . .*'

Reverse angle medium close-up from below. The PRIEST holds out the host to the LITTLE GIRL, but she obstinately keeps her lips tightly closed and shakes her head. (Still on page 68) The PRIEST whispers urgently, off:

PRIEST: *Séverine, Séverine, what's the matter?*

* This section appears in the original script but was not seen in the version screened.

[Suddenly the LITTLE GIRL closes her eyes and falls backwards.

Her body slips on the steps of the communion table and remains motionless. She has fainted. The PRIEST, host in hand, looks at her, very surprised.]*

Resume on SEVERINE on the staircase, the PRIEST's voice still ringing in her ears. Camera pans with her as she reaches the first-floor landing of the building without meeting anyone. Two or three doors, all similar, give onto the landing. She approaches one door, which gives no sign of where it leads, looks round and then draws away. She passes in front of the second door and stops in front of the third, camera tracking after her.

Medium close-up. Camera tracks in on a small, extremely discreet plate fixed beside the bell, which reads: MME ANAIS — FASHIONS.

Resume on SEVERINE, standing by the door. She is just about to ring when she hears a door open somewhere in the building. Camera tracks left as she draws swiftly away from the door, goes towards the lift and pushes on the button to call it as if she is about to leave. She remains there without moving. We hear footsteps coming down the staircase and a middle-aged WOMAN, carrying a shopping bag, passes without looking at SEVERINE, then continues down the stairs. SEVERINE waits a moment. The sound of the WOMAN's footsteps fades away. The lift arrives, but SEVERINE ignores it. Camera pans back as she returns to Madame Anaïs's door. This time, she rings.

Medium close-up of the door from inside. MADAME ANAIS comes up and looks through the spyhole, then opens the door just as SEVERINE rings a second time, revealing her standing on the doorstep, looking around her as if afraid of being seen. MADAME ANAIS asks in a low voice:

MADAME ANAIS : *What is it?*

SEVERINE hesitant : *I wanted to speak to you . . .*

---

* This section appears in the original script but was not seen in the version screened.

59

MADAME ANAIS : *Come in.*

She opens the door a little more and SEVERINE comes in, removing her dark glasses. She stands in the entrance hall, face to face with MADAME ANAIS. The latter is a woman of about forty, wearing a house-coat, respectable-looking, gentle and smiling. There is nothing aggressive in her make-up or anything vulgar in her manners. In the entrance hall, everything is clean and in moderately good taste. It is not a luxurious flat. It consists of four or five unexceptional rooms, which are furnished with anonymous modern furniture. There are reproductions of engravings on the walls. ANAIS closes the door behind her and looks at the newcomer with the greatest interest.

SEVERINE coming in : *Good morning, madame . . .*

ANAIS smiling : *Good morning . . .*

SEVERINE : *Is it you who . . . is concerned with . . .?*

ANAIS : *I am Madame Anaïs.*

Extremely disturbed, SEVERINE stammers, unable to find her words.

SEVERINE : *I wanted to ask . . . to know . . .*

Seeing the young woman's obvious anxiety, ANAIS nods towards another room, saying :

ANAIS : *Come . . . Let's have a quiet talk . . .* *

SEVERINE moves off to the right, then camera pans right round as ANAIS follows her with an appraising eye. Seen from behind, they enter the living room, which is small and furnished in the same way as the hall (and the rest of the flat, as we shall see later). It is not a room where clients are received, but a rest-room for ANAIS and her girls. It contains armchairs, a small round table which can be used for tea or cards, a drinks trolley, a television set which is switched off at the time, magazines, a few books — everything to pass the time. There are paper

---

* In the original script, Buñuel has the following note : ' In all the sequences which take place in the brothel, a very important character will appear. This is the chambermaid, Pallas. She will be present constantly, turning beds, arranging flowers, doing various jobs and occasionally uttering some enigmatic phrases. She has a daughter called Catherine.'

flowers in the vases and a number of rather elaborate lamps. There is also a small wardrobe, though this is not seen at first as the two women stand talking in the middle of the room.

ANAIS to SEVERINE : *Sit down. Can I get you something?*

SEVERINE looks around her, very interested and embarrassed.

SEVERINE : *No, thank you.*

ANAIS producing a cigarette packet : *A cigarette?*

SEVERINE : *No thank you, I don't smoke.*

ANAIS smiles reassuringly, standing opposite her.

ANAIS : *Don't be frightened. Make yourself at home. I'm just waiting to help you . . . Sit down.*

SEVERINE sits in an armchair.

Medium close-up of the two of them as ANAIS sits down opposite SEVERINE, who is three-quarters back to camera in the foreground. She looks at SEVERINE, without concealing her approval. (Still on page 68)

ANAIS : *You are kind and fresh. That's the type we like here . . .* Sympathetically : *I know that it's a bit difficult at the beginning, but who doesn't need money some time or other?* A pause. She leans forward and takes SEVERINE by the chin. Camera tracks in slightly. *You take half. I take half . . .* She smiles.

High angle medium close-up of SEVERINE, MADAME ANAIS in the foreground.

ANAIS : *. . . I have certain expenses.* She drops her hand from SEVERINE's chin.

SEVERINE ill at ease : *Thank you very much, madame . . . but I must go . . .*

She gets up suddenly and moves towards the door of the room, as if she wanted to run away. Camera tilts up and pans with her. ANAIS, who has got up at the same time and followed her, seizes her by the shoulders, but without any brutality, and holds her back.

ANAIS : *Come, come, now. You're a little bit upset . . .*

With a spontaneous movement, she kisses SEVERINE. She is very affectionate and gentle. She continues :

ANAIS : *I bet it's the first time you've worked? . . .* Getting

61

no reply, she adds: *It's not so awful, you'll see . . . It's a bit early yet, and the girls you'll be working with aren't here . . .* She fiddles with the shoulder of SEVERINE's coat and interjects: *You're going to lose a button.* Then, leaning both hands on SEVERINE's shoulder, she continues: *When would you like to start?*

SEVERINE taken by surprise: *I don't know . . .*

ANAIS gently: *Today?*

SEVERINE: *Yes, perhaps . . . But it would only be . . . the afternoon . . . I've got to go at five . . .* Insisting: *I must.*

ANAIS turns and, with her hand on SEVERINE's shoulder, leads her back to the front door, away from camera, which tracks out slightly at the same time.

ANAIS: *Two to five . . . it's a good time. But you must be on time, otherwise I'll be annoyed . . . But at five you'll be free, I promise . . .*

She opens the door (Still on page 68) and SEVERINE goes out, turning back to say:

SEVERINE: *Goodbye . . . Excuse me.*

ANAIS: *I'll be waiting for you this afternoon . . . At two o'clock.*

She closes the door on SEVERINE and comes back towards camera, lighting a cigarette. She looks very satisfied.

[Exterior shot of the courtyard of PIERRE's hospital. It is one hour later and SEVERINE is dressed the same as in the preceding scene. She arrives hurriedly in the courtyard of the hospital and goes up to the PORTER and asks:

SEVERINE: *Is Dr. Sérizy still there?*

The PORTER, his mouth full, points impolitely towards the courtyard, without saying anything.

SEVERINE going away: *Thank you . . .*]*

Low angle medium shot tracking with PIERRE, dressed in a white overall with an overcoat draped over his shoulders, as he crosses the courtyard of the hospital with a group of other doctors.** (Still on page 68) An ambulance

---

* This section appears in the original script but was not seen in the version screened.

** Buñuel's note: ' Beside him are Professor Henri and the medical student whom we shall see again at the end of the film.'

62

moves away off-screen, sounding its siren. PIERRE notices SEVERINE off-screen and appears surprised, even a little anxious as if he expected bad news. He is not used to seeing his wife at the hospital. He leaves his colleagues and comes towards her, camera still tracking with him. He notices that she is a little disturbed and breathless, as if she had been running.

PIERRE : *What's the matter? Nothing serious?*

SEVERINE : *No . . . I . . . was shopping very near here, and I suddenly felt I wanted to see you . . .*

PIERRE, reassured, smiles.

PIERRE : *I thought you didn't like hospitals . . .*

SEVERINE : *No, I don't like them.*

She lays a hand anxiously on his chest. She has come to look for help against some ill-defined threat.

SEVERINE : *I don't want to be alone.* She continues hurriedly : *I'll take you out to lunch.*

Somewhat embarrassed, PIERRE puts an arm round her as he replies :

PIERRE : *I can't, I've got to lunch with the chief . . .* He makes a discreet gesture towards his colleagues in the background. *I told you this morning . . .*

SEVERINE : *Yes, I know, but . . .* [*Can't you get out of it?*

PIERRE : *Yes, of course . . . But it's a bit late . . .*

SEVERINE : *You're right.*

She moves away a step and bows her head slightly. PIERRE tries to comfort her.]*

PIERRE : *I'm sorry . . . But you know that we're going out with the Févrets this evening?*

SEVERINE : *Yes, yes . . .* She makes an effort to smile and adds : *I'm sorry to have bothered you . . .*

PIERRE with a smile : *Bothered me! . . . See you tonight. I'll try to get home as early as possible.*

She suddenly lays her hand anxiously on his chest again, as if seeking his help, and exclaims :

SEVERINE : *Pierre!*

He looks at her for a moment, then leads her away

---

* This section, which appears in the original script, was not included in the film.

63

towards the hospital entrance, camera panning slightly with them. Then he kisses her on both cheeks and goes off to the left as SEVERINE goes out into the street. (Still on page 68)

[Exterior shot of a public park, daytime. A woman is sitting on a bench. In one hand she is holding a book, which she is reading. With the other hand, she is gently rocking a pram. She stops the rocking to turn a page of the book. Then she starts again. SEVERINE sits down beside her and glances distractedly towards the pram where a child is sleeping. Then she remains motionless, looking fixedly at the ground. There are tears in her eyes.]*

High angle medium shot of the staircase at ANAIS's. Only SEVERINE's feet are visible as they come hesitantly up the stairs. At the first landing they halt, turn back, then turn and move on again, camera tilting to follow them up to the next flight. (Still on page 68)

Medium close-up of the nameplate and bell push outside ANAIS's. SEVERINE's hand comes into shot and pushes on the bell. Camera tracks to include SEVERINE and pans left as she moves away from the door and takes off her sunglasses. The door opens, off-screen. Camera pans back as SEVERINE moves across to the open door. MADAME ANAIS is standing there. Suddenly her face breaks into a smile.

ANAIS : *Well, I wasn't expecting to see you again! You left so suddenly this morning . . . I thought I'd frightened you . . .* She beckons her in with a nod of her head. *Come in.*

SEVERINE goes in and ANAIS shuts the door behind her.

Medium shot of the wardrobe in ANAIS's living room. ANAIS enters shot, opens the doors and says to SEVERINE off-screen :

ANAIS : *You can put your things in here . . .*

She takes out a coat-hanger and comes back towards SEVERINE, camera panning with her. SEVERINE removes

---

* This section in square brackets, taken from the original script, does not occur at this point in the film but would seem to partially match the two shots which precede Séverine's first visit to the brothel.

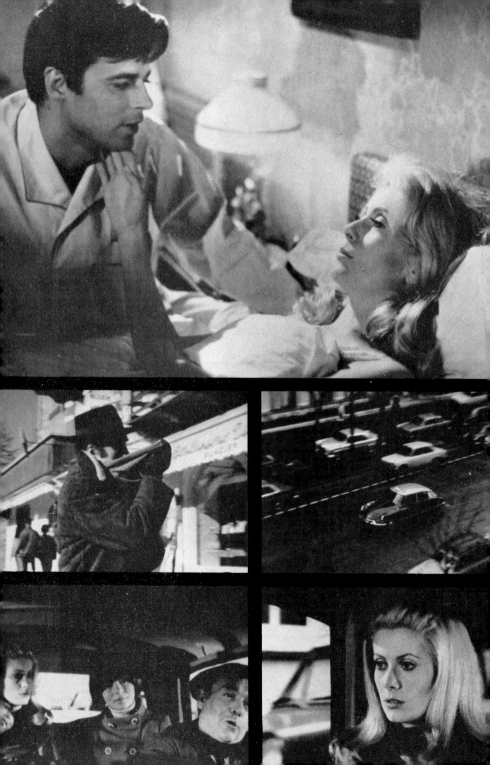

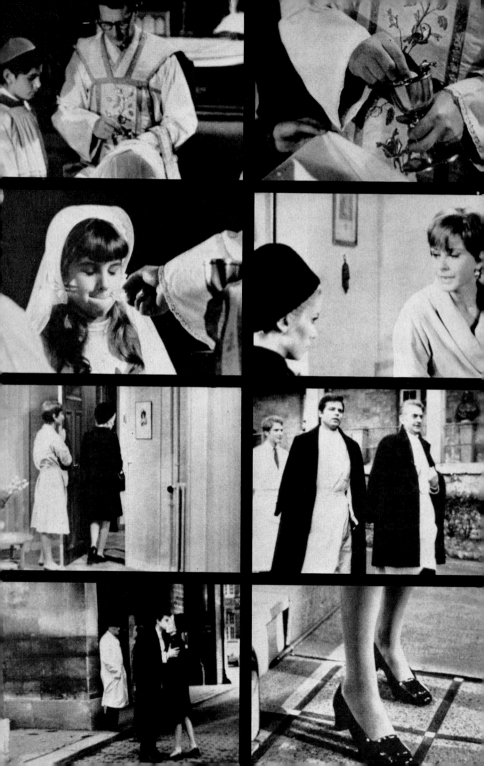

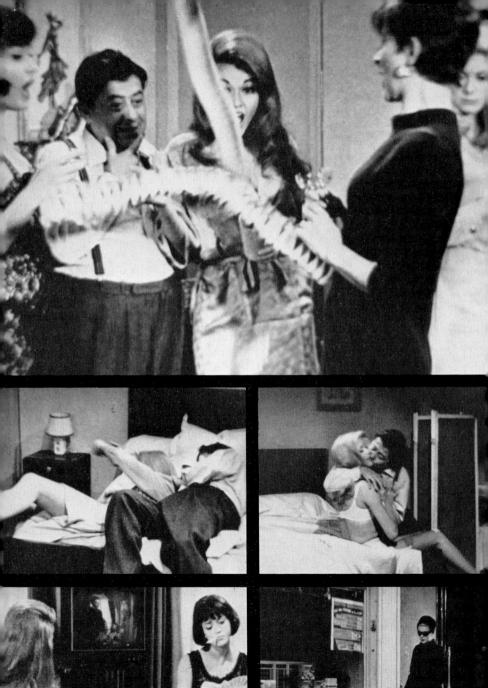

her coat, which ANAIS takes and puts on the hanger. She
is wearing a tailored dress underneath. She starts to take
off her gloves as ANAIS continues:

ANAIS: *You'll see your colleagues soon. There are two at
present, Mathilde and Charlotte. Both of them are very nice.
In any case, I only like people who have been well brought up
. . .* She wags a finger at SEVERINE . . . *and they must be
cheerful!* As she continues, she walks across to the wardrobe
to hang up SEVERINE's coat, camera panning with her. *You've
got to like your work . . .* She closes the wardrobe and comes
back towards SEVERINE again. *Last week, I had to sack Maité,
though she was a very good-looking girl. But she was really too
rude . . . Pity . . .*

The two women are now standing at the door of the
living room. ANAIS points into the room and says:

ANAIS: *Come in.* They go out of shot.

Medium close-up of SEVERINE as she sits down on a chair
in the living room. On the table in front of her are a
champagne bottle and several glasses — ANAIS addresses
her from off-screen.

ANAIS: *What's your name?*

SEVERINE looking up, embarrassed: *I wouldn't like . . .*

Close-up of the drinks trolley. We see ANAIS's hands
ladling cherries in brandy from a preserving jar as she
addresses SEVERINE off-screen.

ANAIS laughing: *I'm not asking for your real name! You
don't really think I'm called Anaïs! . . . We'll have something to celebrate your arrival.*

SEVERINE off: *No thank you, madame.*

ANAIS: *Oh, you must . . . A little cherry in brandy.*

Camera tilts up to ANAIS's face. She goes across to a
table at the side of the room and picks up a glass of
brandy for herself as she continues:

ANAIS: *We must choose a simple, smart name for you, easy
to remember . . . We can choose together, if you like . . .*

Resume on SEVERINE, seated. At that moment, from
another room in the flat, we hear women's laughter,
dominated by a man's laugh which sounds rather coarse
and loud. SEVERINE, who is just taking off her hat, listens.

73

Resume on ANAIS, standing on the other side of the room. She examines SEVERINE's reactions, smiling, and explains reassuringly:

ANAIS : *We call him Monsieur Adolphe. He's one of our best clients. He's very funny, you'll find* . . .

Camera pans with her as she comes back and sits down beside SEVERINE.

ANAIS : *I've had an idea: what if we called you Belle de Jour?*
SEVERINE absently : *Belle de Jour?*
ANAIS : *Because you only come in the afternoon* . . .
SEVERINE : *If you like, yes* . . .

High angle medium close-up of ANAIS and SEVERINE, who is three-quarters back to camera. ANAIS puts down her glass of brandy and leans forward on the armchair where SEVERINE is sitting. Camera moves slowly round to show the two of them in profile. SEVERINE is nervously holding her glass of brandied cherries.

ANAIS : *You look a bit nervous. Relax. You'll be out at five o'clock, don't worry* . . . Lowering her voice and caressing SEVERINE's fingers : *Is someone waiting for you?* . . . *A boy friend?* . . . *A husband?* . . .

SEVERINE withdraws her hand nervously. ANAIS calms her immediately.

ANAIS : *Don't think I'm trying to get things out of you* . . . *Give me a kiss* . . . . (Still on page 69)

She leans towards SEVERINE and kisses her gently on the lips. SEVERINE starts back, shocked, but not, we feel, necessarily displeased. At that moment several knocks are heard against a partition, accompanied by raucous laughter from the girls and MONSIEUR ADOLPHE. ANAIS says :

ANAIS : *Aha! The girls are thirsty* . . . She gets up and says to SEVERINE : *Wait here, I'm coming back.*

She goes out. SEVERINE sits alone, looking rather lost. She puts down her glass, which is still almost full, then undoes her hair and shakes it loose with a jerk of her head.

General shot of the living room, with the open doorway leading to the rest of the apartment in the background.

Severine sits in the foreground, back to camera, and listens to the noises which reach her from the other rooms in the flat: Anais's step, a door opening, Anais's voice (too low to hear what she is saying), women's cries and, dominating everything, Monsieur Adolphe's voice shouting:

Monsieur Adolphe off: *A new one, and you're hiding her from me!*

Severine gets up and walks slowly towards the doorway as Monsieur Adolphe continues:

Monsieur Adolphe: *Come on then, bring her quick, or I'll fetch her myself!*

Hearing these words, Severine pauses, hurries back to a sofa in the foreground and picks up her hat and bag, then goes across to the wardrobe. She opens the door, as if she was going to take her clothes to get away. Camera pans slightly to follow her. At that moment Anais's voice is heard off:

Anais: *Belle!*

Severine hastily shuts the wardrobe, and camera pans as she goes back towards the doorway, still clutching her hat and bag. Anais appears in the doorway and calmly takes Severine's hat and bag from her, putting them down on a chest of drawers at the side of the room as she continues:

Anais: *You'll find he's very funny. He's a sweet manufacturer. He has factories at Bordeaux and he's very rich . . . Come on . . .* She takes Severine by the hand and leads her from the room.

[Anais, holding Severine by the arm, guides her across the entrance hall, then, without saying anything, along the corridor to the door of the room called the Blue Room. Anais then lets Severine pass in front of her. The door of the room is open.]*

Medium shot of one of the prostitutes, Mathilde, dressing behind a screen in the Blue Room. She is the one whom Severine saw in the street; a very quiet girl, a

---

* This section, which appears in the original script, was not seen in the version screened.

little older than CHARLOTTE, a brunette, very obedient and reserved. Camera pans left to show MONSIEUR ADOLPHE and CHARLOTTE. MONSIEUR ADOLPHE, who is about forty or fifty, is small, paunchy, vulgar and always ready to make some stupid remark. He is dressed in shirt and trousers and is wearing braces. He is slightly drunk and is smoking a cigar. He is holding CHARLOTTE on his knee, caressing her. She is a young, cheerful, good-looking girl, wearing a black and flesh-coloured frilled corset. She laughs when MONSIEUR ADOLPHE tickles her. (Still on page 69)

MONSIEUR ADOLPHE : *If I don't make it some nights, I can always go for a run to send me to sleep.* CHARLOTTE laughs gaily and tweaks his nose. *I went with a Negress the other night in Brussels . . . What a time I had!*

Medium shot of the doorway. ANAIS appears with SEVERINE and brings her into the room. Camera tracks out in front of them to include MONSIEUR ADOLPHE and CHARLOTTE.

ANAIS : *I want to introduce Belle de Jour!*

SEVERINE hardly dares to look the other two women and MONSIEUR ADOLPHE in the face. She is extremely embarrassed.

CHARLOTTE and MATHILDE friendly : *Hello . . .*

SEVERINE very quietly : *Hello . . .*

ANAIS : *I told you to close that curtain.*

She goes off to the right. MONSIEUR ADOLPHE looks at his watch, very pleased with himself :

MONSIEUR ADOLPHE : *Belle de Jour, I pay my respects of a quarter to three . . . You'll have a glass of champagne with us . . .* To ANAIS : *Anaïs, love, a bottle, and make it snappy.*

Close-up of SEVERINE, who looks at him, stupefied. She is completely taken aback.

CHARLOTTE off : *You're lucky. They always open a bottle for a new girl . . .*

MATHILDE to MONSIEUR ADOLPHE : *It sounds as if you've had a sniff of it already!*

Low angle medium shot of ANAIS drawing the curtains in front of the window. Camera pans left as she comes back across the room.

ANAIS : *Get acquainted. I'll be right back.*

As she passes in front of MONSIEUR ADOLPHE, who still has CHARLOTTE on his knee, he pinches her behind . . . She exclaims and moves off to get the champagne. MONSIEUR ADOLPHE gazes after her lustfully as we hear her calling to the maid off. (ANAIS is in fact still a very attractive woman.)

ANAIS off : *Pallas!*

MONSIEUR ADOLPHE : *A bloody fine woman! . . . Nothing wrong with her . . . it's all real.*

CHARLOTTE, who guesses his intentions, says :

CHARLOTTE : *Forget it. I've told you . . . She's much too high-class . . .*

MONSIEUR ADOLPHE : *That's exactly why, love.*

He hugs her close to him and kisses her breasts, then claps her on the behind.

CHARLOTTE : *Just listen to him! Never gives up!*

CHARLOTTE gets off MONSIEUR ADOLPHE's knees, and camera tilts up and pans left as she goes up to SEVERINE, who is watching the proceedings uncertainly. CHARLOTTE looks at her *haute couture* dress and says :

CHARLOTTE to SEVERINE : *It's very pretty, that . . . But you ought to wear something you can do a quick strip in.* Turning towards MONSIEUR ADOLPHE : *Isn't that so, Monsieur Adolphe?*

Medium close-up of MONSIEUR ADOLPHE, who is observing SEVERINE closely while chewing on his cigar. He doesn't think so, and says :

MONSIEUR ADOLPHE : *Oh no, not at all! I think she's a knock-out in her pretty little dress. She looks refined. I like that.*

MATHILDE, who has approached from the background, now wearing a blue dressing gown, kneels down beside MONSIEUR ADOLPHE.

MATHILDE : *You've been promising me a present for God knows how long . . . Well, I'd like something like that!* She nods towards SEVERINE's dress.

MONSIEUR ADOLPHE : *I'm not Rothschild, love!*

MATHILDE : *Worse luck.*

Camera tilts up and pans left with MATHILDE as she goes towards SEVERINE and examines the dress more closely.

MATHILDE : *What a beautiful cut . . . look how well finished it is.*

CHARLOTTE hitching up her corset : *Huh! When you've got the dough it's easy to be well-dressed.*

MONSIEUR ADOLPHE off : *What about class? You can't buy that!*

ANAIS returns, carrying a bottle of champagne in an ice-bucket, followed by PALLAS with a tray of glasses.

ANAIS : *Here's the champagne.*

She is greeted by general cries of satisfaction. Camera pans right and tilts down as they put the champagne and the glasses in front of MONSIEUR ADOLPHE.

MONSIEUR ADOLPHE : *Ah! I was beginning to feel thirsty . . .*

High angle medium shot of the group. ANAIS turns to talk to SEVERINE and CHARLOTTE in the foreground, while PALLAS starts undoing the wire surrounding the cork. MONSIEUR ADOLPHE then gets up and takes the bottle from her.

MONSIEUR ADOLPHE to PALLAS : *Give that to me, it's a man's job. I'm the world's champion cork-popper, didn't you know?*

CHARLOTTE : *Well, you've had plenty of practice.*

He laughs again and sets to work, while PALLAS goes off. While he works, MONSIEUR ADOLPHE starts to sing boisterously.

MONSIEUR ADOLPHE singing : ' *I like ham and sausages,*
*I like ham when it's good*
*But I'd much rather have*
*A nice pair of thighs . . .'*

The cork jumps in his face right in the middle of his song. The froth goes everywhere. CHARLOTTE and MATHILDE squeal. CHARLOTTE, who has been standing with her arm round SEVERINE, goes over to pick up the glasses as he fills them.

MONSIEUR ADOLPHE complaining loudly : *It's because it's not chilled enough . . . over eight degrees champagne is like tea.*

ANAIS : *I'm very sorry. If I'd known I'd have put the bottle in the fridge.*

CHARLOTTE hands round the glasses.

MONSIEUR ADOLPHE : *But you knew perfectly well I was coming.*

ANAIS looking at SEVERINE : *I didn't know Belle de Jour was.*

MONSIEUR ADOLPHE then raises his glass and shouts, very cheerfully :

MONSIEUR ADOLPHE : *To the dearest health of all: mine!*

They all raise their glasses.

ANAIS looking at SEVERINE : *And to the health of Belle de Jour!*

They all drink. SEVERINE looks and listens with a mixture of astonishment and fear. MONSIEUR ADOLPHE lowers his glass.

MONSIEUR ADOLPHE : *It's good, but a bit warm, huh?*

A shot of MONSIEUR ADOLPHE's jacket hanging on the back of a chair with his shoes neatly arranged underneath. SEVERINE's and CHARLOTTE's legs are seen in the foreground.

MONSIEUR ADOLPHE off at first : *Ah, Mathilde! I've brought you a little present! I almost forgot!*

Camera tilts up as he comes into shot, followed by MATHILDE. He rummages in his jacket pocket, takes a little box out of it and hands it to MATHILDE.

MONSIEUR ADOLPHE : *Here you are . . .*

MATHILDE : *What is it?*

MONSIEUR ADOLPHE : *Have a look . . .*

Everyone looks on curiously, except SEVERINE, who moves away and stands with her back to the group. MONSIEUR ADOLPHE smiles knowingly.

MATHILDE : *Thank you.*

She opens the box, which contains a jack-in-a-box, and a long articulated snake jumps in her face. She shouts out in fright and everyone bursts out laughing. (Still on page 70) MONSIEUR ADOLPHE puts his arms round the two girls and kisses MATHILDE while ANAIS says indulgently :

ANAIS : *He's so amusing . . . He brings some new trick every time . . .*

79

Severine is the only one who does not laugh. Everything she sees seems strange and new to her.

Monsieur Adolphe : *Here's to fun!*

Medium close-up of Monsieur Adolphe with his arms round the two girls.

Monsieur Adolphe : *That's how I am, I like to live. And I want everyone to laugh.*

The girls laugh, then suddenly fall silent as Monsieur Adolphe looks towards Severine off-screen. Camera pans right as he walks across to her. Anais is seen in back view, carefully watching Severine's reactions.

Monsieur Adolphe : *Well, Belle de Jour?* He chucks her under the chin. *What are you pulling faces for?* He walks round to the other side of her; camera pans, cutting out Anais. *What's wrong with you?*

He takes her champagne glass and throws it over his shoulder. It crashes to the floor off-screen. Camera tilts down as he sits her down on the bed and starts to unzip her dress.

Monsieur Adolphe : *You'll see . . . I promise you we'll have a good time together.* (Still on page 70)

He opens her dress and forces her back onto the bed. With a cry, Severine frees herself and rushes off. Camera tilts up as Monsieur Adolphe rises to his feet, very surprised. He asks Anais :

Monsieur Adolphe : *What's the matter with her?*

Anais appears, comes up to Monsieur Adolphe and says in a very low voice :

Anais : *I'll take her out for a minute. You mustn't rush her . . . It's her first time.*

Monsieur Adolphe incredulous : *I've heard that one before.*

Anais : *It's true. I swear it.*

She hands her glass to Monsieur Adolphe and camera pans left as she goes out past the now silent girls into the corridor.

Medium shot of Anais from behind. Camera pans slightly as she goes down the corridor towards Severine, who is standing with her back to us.

Monsieur Adolphe off : *She's crazy. Who does she think she is, the little bitch!*

MATHILDE off : *Oh, she's new.*

ANAIS puts her arm round SEVERINE's shoulder and leads her slowly back towards camera.

ANAIS smiling : *That's very good. You've made a hit already. Monsieur Adolphe is a simple man, so don't upset yourself. Just do what he wants, that's all he asks.*

SEVERINE, who has listened with a sort of anxiety, makes a sudden movement towards the entrance hall and says :

SEVERINE : *No. I want to leave. Let me go.*

ANAIS : *What?*

ANAIS stands in SEVERINE's way, seizes her brutally by her arm and forces her to stay there. She says to her in a voice that has changed completely, suddenly very hard and contemptuous :

ANAIS : *All right, come on. How much longer are you going to go on playing this game? Where d'you think you are?* Camera pans slightly as she pushes her towards the room. *Go on!*

SEVERINE stands with a strange expression, as if all her fear and her wish to get away had suddenly disappeared. It almost looks as though she expected to be treated like this, as though she wanted it.

SEVERINE in an obedient voice : *Yes, I'm going, madame . . . I'm going.*

MONSIEUR ADOLPHE off : *Leave me alone with her.*

ANAIS : *What you need is a firm hand. Is that it?*

Camera tracks out as CHARLOTTE and MATHILDE come out of the doorway and pass in front of SEVERINE without a word. Pan slightly right, cutting out ANAIS, as SEVERINE moves forward and hesitates in the doorway.

ANAIS off : *Go on!* She goes in.

Medium shot inside the room. MONSIEUR ADOLPHE is standing wiping his face on a towel by the wash-basin in the corner. The curtains are drawn and the lights are on.

MONSIEUR ADOLPHE : *Ah . . . hello.* He turns out the light over the basin. *Close the door.*

SEVERINE closes the door behind her. Camera pans left as he comes past the end of the double bed towards

81

SEVERINE. He starts undoing her dress as he speaks to her :

MONSIEUR ADOLPHE : *I've sent the others away . . . It'll be more intimate . . .*

She stands stiffly as he unzips the front of her dress and says :

MONSIEUR ADOLPHE : *It seems it's your first time?* Camera pans and tracks round as he sits on the bed and draws her towards him. *Be careful though!* He wags his finger at her. *I've got a nose for that kind of thing. Don't tell me any lies.* He strips off her dress and looks appraisingly at her body. *Mind you, if it's true there's no need to be ashamed.*

SEVERINE begins to look round with a mixture of desperation and bewilderment, as he gets up and pulls her close to him.

MONSIEUR ADOLPHE : *You're not going to tell me that you're still a virgin, at your age . . . eh? In any case, we'll soon find out.*

He tries to kiss her, but she resists. She looks at him as though this man really inspires horror in her. Camera pans as she pulls away from him and sits on the side of the bed. MONSIEUR ADOLPHE follows her and stands over her looking astonished.

MONSIEUR ADOLPHE gently : *Well? Is it me you're frightened of? Is it my face you don't like?* His tone hardens as he says : *You'll have to get used to it, my pet.* (Still on page 70)

He kisses her and pushes her down onto the bed. She gasps, then struggles free and rushes across the room towards the door, pursued by MONSIEUR ADOLPHE.

Medium shot of the bottom half of the door. We see SEVERINE'S legs as she rushes towards it and wrenches it open. MONSIEUR ADOLPHE catches her, furious with her for resisting. Camera tilts up and pans right as he grabs her arms and pushes her away from the door, shouting at her angrily.

MONSIEUR ADOLPHE : *Oh no! You're not getting away like that.*

Still struggling with her, he pushes her towards the bed and insults her :

MONSIEUR ADOLPHE : *Who d'you think you are, you little slut?* He slaps her face. *Leading me on and then stopping me . . . You can play at being uppish for a bit . . . I've had enough.*

He throws her brutally on the bed. Camera tilts down with her. She falls and stays motionless. Camera tilts up to MONSIEUR ADOLPHE again as he stops, a little out of breath. He looks at her and smiles, triumphant.

MONSIEUR ADOLPHE : *There, that's better . . .* He shrugs off his braces, letting fall his trousers. *What you need is a bit of the rough stuff, eh?*

Then he leans over her, camera tilting down again. He falls on her and kisses her roughly. She does not resist any more.

General shot of the living room. At first we see MATHILDE and CHARLOTTE, then camera tracks out to include ANAIS. They are all seated round the table. The television is on in the background. CHARLOTTE and ANAIS are playing gin rummy and MATHILDE is sewing. CHARLOTTE throws down a card. (Still on page 70)

CHARLOTTE : *Jack of clubs.*

ANAIS off at first : *Jack of clubs . . . my gin card.*

She pours herself a brandy from the drinks trolley in the foreground.

ANAIS raising her glass : *Adolphe is taking his time . . .*

MATHILDE : *He always does.*

They all laugh. ANAIS puts down her glass and picks up a card, then lays down her hand saying triumphantly :

ANAIS : *Gin!*

CHARLOTTE exclaims in mock despair.

Medium shot as SEVERINE leaves the apartment block where ANAIS lives. It is nearly five o'clock. As she comes out she stops for a moment on the threshold, and looks rapidly to right and left. Then, putting on her sunglasses, she walks away rapidly along the pavement, camera tracking with her as she passes the dairy and goes off out of sight round the corner. (Still on page 70)

Back at home, the same day, SEVERINE has undressed

and is taking a shower. We see her through the frosted glass of the shower cabinet. She rubs her neck and shoulders vigorously, then bends down to wash the rest of her body, camera tilting down with her. She puts a lot of energy and application into this, as if she wanted to rid her body of any suspicious smell. Camera pans away from the shower cabinet, past a towel hanging over the bath and then on to the wash-basin with its flasks of perfume. Another similar shot of the bathroom. Camera pans back again, tilting up to show SEVERINE who has now emerged from the shower wearing her pink bathrobe and a pink towel around her head. She stands in front of the wash-basin and picks up her lipstick. Camera pans across to her reflection in the mirror as she applies it. Still reflected in the mirror, we see her turn and pick up her brassière from a chair behind her. Camera tilts down as she picks up the rest of her underwear from a stool in the foreground.

Medium shot of SEVERINE coming through the deserted apartment, carrying her underwear. Camera pans right round to show her from behind as she goes into the drawing room, where a wood fire is burning. Then it tracks in as she sits down beside the fireplace and throws her underclothes and stockings into it; they catch fire immediately. (Still on page 71) As they burn, she pushes them down with the poker, then she hears the front door of the apartment open. Suddenly, as if afraid, she leaves the drawing room and runs towards her bedroom, camera panning after her.

High angle shot of her bed. Camera tilts up as she runs into the room, turns out the light, lies down quickly and pulls the blankets over her. Pretending to be asleep, she closes her eyes, does not move and breathes calmly. PIERRE's voice can be heard in the drawing room. He has just come in and is looking for his wife.

PIERRE off : *Séverine, where are you? . . . Are you ready?*

She does not reply and remains motionless. PIERRE comes into the bedroom, turns on the light and is astonished to see his wife in bed.

PIERRE lowering his voice: *Ah! You're there, are you? What's the matter with you? Something wrong?* Anxious, he approaches her and sits on the edge of the bed. *Are you ill?*

Medium close-up of SEVERINE with PIERRE sitting beside her on the bed. He puts his hand on her forehead. She opens her eyes as if she had just woken up.

PIERRE: *You don't seem to have a temperature . . . Do you want me to send for somebody?*

SEVERINE: *No, no, there's nothing wrong . . . I was asleep. I had a headache, I don't know why . . . I took an aspirin and a hot bath. I'll feel better tomorrow . . . What time is it?*

PIERRE looks at his watch.

PIERRE: *It's late. I'll telephone the Févrets to tell them not to wait for us.*

SEVERINE: *You can go by yourself . . .*

PIERRE: *Certainly not. I'll be a lot better here. Anyway, I've got some work to do.* He kisses her on the forehead, gently, and says: *Have a rest. Good night.*

He moves away. SEVERINE has closed her eyes and she looks as though she is sleeping again. PIERRE then switches off the light, goes out noiselessly and closes the bedroom door. Camera tracks in to close-up of SEVERINE's face. She opens her eyes and presses her hands to her forehead. We hear the sound of cow-bells off.

Long shot of a meadow in the Camargue. Camera tracks sideways with a herd of wild bulls as they pass at a gallop with a ringing of bells and a thunder of hooves. They are led by three herdsmen on horseback. Camera halts and the herd gallops off on either side of the frame.

High angle medium close-up of a cooking-pot of soup boiling away vigorously on a fire which has been lit between several large stones. (Still on page 71) PIERRE's legs appear as HUSSON's voice asks:

HUSSON off: *Is the soup ready?*

PIERRE bends down and takes a spoonful. Camera tilts up to his face as he tastes it. The herd of bulls bellow in the background.

PIERRE : *It's cold. And I can't warm it up again.**

Camera pans with PIERRE as he goes to pick up a spade and comes back towards the fire. This time we see HUSSON seated beside it drinking a bowl of soup. PIERRE leans on the spade and points to the herd in the background.

PIERRE : *Do they give bulls names as they do with cats?*

HUSSON : *Yes. Most of those are called Remorse . . .* He glances at the bulls and turns back to his soup . . . *except for the last one, which is called Expiation.*

A church bell is heard tolling in the distance. PIERRE leans his chin on the handle of his spade and gazes at the ground while HUSSON stands up, throws away his soup bowl, takes off his hat and stands with his head bowed. (Still on page 72)

Low angle medium close-up of HUSSON with lowered eyes. The church bell continues to toll while the bulls bellow loudly.

**[HUSSON sings a snatch of his favourite song :

HUSSON : *' I like ham and sausages,*
*I like ham when it's good . . .'*

PIERRE looks towards the sky and says :

PIERRE : *The weather's breaking up . . .*

HUSSON : *It's going to rain.*

Great black clouds gather together overhead; there are lightning flashes followed by a clap of thunder. PIERRE holds out his hand. The first drops of rain are beginning to fall.

---

* In the original script, this piece of dialogue is preceded by the follow-ing note: 'A number of substitutions of words and other significant linguistic mistakes will be noticed in their dialogue.' In fact Pierre's reference to the soup is an untranslatable play on words. In French the word ' soup ' is feminine, thus ' it's cold ' etc. becomes ' she's cold ' etc., referring both to the soup and, implicitly, to Séverine. Another feature of this scene is that although we hear Pierre's and Husson's voices, at no time do we see their lips move.

** In the original script, this section in square brackets follows straight on from Pierre's comment about the soup; in the film it is substituted by the mud-slinging episode. The song which ' Husson ' sings reflects the fact that originally Pierre's partner in this whole episode was Monsieur Adolphe; however, in the copy of the original script on which this version is based, the name is already partially changed to Husson, and we have therefore used the latter name for the sake of continuity.

PIERRE : *It's beginning to ' expiate '* . . .

HUSSON : *Father, forgive them, for they know not what they do . . . Come on, quick, before it really starts to come down . . . Help me.*

They put their plates down, get up quickly and wrap their hands up in the scarves they have been wearing round their necks. Their hands protected by the scarves, they seize the heavy pot of steaming soup and move away several steps. The rain falls twice as heavily. The lightning and the thunder occur with increasing frequency. At that moment we see SEVERINE tied to a tree dressed the same (with her dress partly torn off) and in the same position as in the first sequence of the film in the Bois de Boulogne. The two men lift the pot, not without some effort, and pour the contents over SEVERINE's head and shoulders.

HUSSON : *You see, Séverine, how well he can look after you when he wants.*

The young woman's body, which has been burnt, turns red. It gives off a lot of steam. SEVERINE utters a piercing cry of pain. But on her face, an expression of pleasure clearly appears.]

High angle medium shot of the two men's legs as HUSSON shovels thick black mud into a bucket. (Still on page 72)

HUSSON : *What's the time?*

PIERRE : *Between two and five, but not later than five.*

HUSSON : *And how is your wife?*

PIERRE : *Very well, thank you.*

HUSSON : *Where is she?*

PIERRE : *Over there perhaps. Do you want to say hello?*

HUSSON : *With pleasure.*

Medium shot of SEVERINE standing in a dilapidated open cattle shed. Her hands are tied in a similar position as in the first sequence of the film in the Bois de Boulogne. She is wearing a long white sleeveless robe. (Still on page 72) Camera tracks in on her as HUSSON is heard insulting her off :

HUSSON off : *How are you, you little piece of trash?* . . . Camera tracks in on her further . . . *Feeling all right, slut?* A handful of mud hits her virginal white robe, hurled by

Husson off-screen . . . *Scum!* . . . More mud hits her . . . *Swill!* . . . *Rubbish!* . . . *Sodomite!* . . . Her face and neck are gradually covered by the mud.

Medium shot of Husson hurling the mud while Pierre stands impassively looking on. (Still on page 72)

Husson : *Dung devourer!*

Close-up of Severine, now completely plastered with mud. She stands passively as more mud hits her, and her voice is heard crying out (though her lips do not move):

Severine : *Pierre! Pierre! Please stop. I love you!*

(Still on page 72)

[The scene changes to the living room at Anais's, day-time. Anais is leafing through a magazine, sipping a drink. Charlotte is darning. Mathilde is playing patience. Everything is peaceful. At that moment the front door bell rings. Anais gets up, glancing at the clock, and says :

Anais : *The Professor is early* . . .

She puts her magazine down and goes into the entrance hall.]*

Medium close-up of Anais's front door from inside. It swings open to reveal Severine standing on the doorstep wearing dark glasses. Anais's voice addresses her coldly off.

Anais : *What do you want?*

Severine takes off her dark glasses and says hesitantly :

Severine : *I wanted* . . .

Medium close-up of Anais in profile standing at the door with Severine off-screen outside. Taken aback by this welcome, Severine does not know what to reply.

Severine off : *I* . . . *I wanted* . . .

Anais : . . . *to have your job back? And then disappear again for a week? Without saying a thing?*

Severine off : *I'm sorry, I* . . .

Anais interrupting her abruptly again : *I don't want any amateur work here. There's the street for that.*

She tries to close the door. Severine appears, places her

---

* This section appears in the original script but was not seen in the version screened.

hand on the door as if to prevent ANAIS from closing it.

SEVERINE begging : *Please, madame . . .*

ANAIS allows herself to weaken.

ANAIS : *You're lucky it's me you're dealing with. I know plenty who'd have thrown you out, and no messing about . . .*

Sighing, she lets SEVERINE come in and closes the door behind her. Camera pans as SEVERINE advances into the hall.

ANAIS : *But I'm too kind-hearted . . .* Camera pans again as she comes round SEVERINE . . . *But if you come back, you must work properly.*

SEVERINE : *Yes . . .*

ANAIS : *I can rely on you every day?*

SEVERINE : *Yes, but only till five o'clock . . .*

ANAIS : *All right . . . go on.*

She jerks her head towards the living room. Camera pans left as SEVERINE does as she is told.

General shot of the living room. CHARLOTTE is seated in the foreground playing patience, with MATHILDE beside her. In the background PALLAS opens the living room door and SEVERINE comes in, followed by ANAIS.

PALLAS : *Good afternoon, madame. It's very nice to see you again.*

SEVERINE : *Hello.*

She comes towards the table. CHARLOTTE and MATHILDE seem pleased to see SEVERINE again. ANAIS stands watching her sternly in the background.

MATHILDE : *Hello, how are you?*

CHARLOTTE looking up without stopping her game : *Well, it's Belle de Jour. How are you?*

SEVERINE : *Very well, thank you.*

CHARLOTTE : *You ran out on us.*

MATHILDE : *Why didn't you come back sooner?*

SEVERINE starting to take off her coat : *I couldn't.*

MATHILDE getting up to help SEVERINE take off her coat : *Give me your coat.*

SEVERINE : *Thank you.*

Camera tracks in, cutting out CHARLOTTE, while ANAIS sits down on the arm of MATHILDE's chair.

89

MATHILDE looking at SEVERINE'S coat: *Isn't it pretty! I say, would you do me a favour? You couldn't lend it to me for Sunday? I'll give it back to you on Monday.*

SEVERINE having taken off her hat puts it down on the tables and replies, rather embarrassed:

SEVERINE: *Well, I hate to refuse but Sunday is a little difficult . . . I can't . . .*

Camera pans left as MATHILDE goes to hang the coat in the wardrobe and CHARLOTTE steps forward and helps SEVERINE off with her dress. As she does so she says to MATHILDE:

CHARLOTTE: *Don't worry. I've seen the same ready-made.*

In the background MATHILDE holds up the coat, sees the label and exclaims:

MATHILDE: *Carducci! . . . You don't go short of anything . . .*

CHARLOTTE curiously: *Who are you?*

SEVERINE does not answer. Camera tracks out, including ANAIS again, as MATHILDE returns from the wardrobe carrying a dressing gown. CHARLOTTE goes to hang up her dress.

MATHILDE: *Are you sad to be back?*

SEVERINE: *No.*

MATHILDE: *I'm here because of my fiancé. He had an accident, so he can't work. He knows I come here. But I love him a lot . . .*

SEVERINE takes off her petticoat and MATHILDE helps her on with the dressing gown.

MATHILDE: *Of course, I could make a living somewhere else.*

ANAIS getting up and interrupting her: *But what would you make?*

MATHILDE: *That's true.*

Coming round the table, ANAIS sits facing SEVERINE with her back to camera.

ANAIS: *We're expecting the Professor any minute . . . As if she has suddenly had an idea: I'll introduce you to him. You're just his type.*

SEVERINE: *Who is he?*

ANAIS: *A women's doctor. Quite famous, I believe.*

MATHILDE: *His patients come from all over the world.*

The bell on the front door rings, very discreetly. Anais gets up and says :

Anais : *There he is.*

Before going out, she points to Severine and says to Charlotte :

Anais : *Tell her a bit about it.*

Charlotte : *Yes, madame.*

Anais goes out to open the door for the Professor. Camera pans left with Charlotte as she goes over to the standard lamp at the side of the room and turns it on, saying :

Charlotte : *We need the light on already* . . . Camera pans back again as she goes across to Severine and says : *You'll see, it's not very difficult . . . If they were all like him!* . . . *Anyway* . . .

We cut just as Charlotte is going to start her explanation.

[In the entrance hall of the apartment, Anais asks the Professor to come in.

Anais : *Good afternoon.*

Professor : *Good afternoon, madame.*

He is a man of about fifty, grey-haired, but still handsome and looks very well cared-for. He is carrying a black case in his hand.

Anais : *Come in . . .*]*

General shot of the corridor. Anais precedes the Professor along the corridor as far as the door of the Pink Room and says to him as they walk :

Anais : *I've got someone new.*

Professor interested : *Ah?*

Anais : *I think you'll like her very much. Perhaps a little shy. But a real aristocrat.*

Professor stopping, suspicious : *Really?*

Anais : *Come come now* . . .

Professor : *Very well, then. Send her to me.*

Anais : *Please go in.*

The Professor goes into the Pink Room while Madame

---

* This section was not seen in the version screened.

ANAIS comes back into the corridor and advances towards camera.

Medium shot of the PROFESSOR inside the Pink Room. He takes off his hat and hangs it on the back of the door. He comes towards camera and inspects his gums in the mirror before hanging up his coat also. (Still on page 105) Camera tracks as he takes his black case and goes into the bathroom, which adjoins the Pink Room. He places his case on a stool in the bathroom, opens it and takes out a braided cap; it is rather like those caps sported by hotel porters. He dusts it off, adjusts it on his head and looks at himself in the mirror. (Still on page 105) He doesn't like it. He takes the cap off with a sudden movement, and, apparently dissatisfied, throws it into the case. Camera tilts down to show the contents of the case, which include a leather thonged scourge which he picks up and hangs over his arm. There are various other unidentifiable props in the case.

Medium shot of SEVERINE in back view as she comes into the Pink Room and closes the door. She looks round uncertainly, hearing metallic noises in the bathroom where the PROFESSOR is. Camera follows her as she goes and peers through the bathroom door, which is slightly ajar. Not knowing exactly what she has to do, she goes over to the bed and starts to undress. First of all she removes her bathrobe, then her brassière. The bathroom door opens quietly and the PROFESSOR appears. He sees SEVERINE undressing and asks her, with a very angry look :

PROFESSOR : *What are you doing?* (Still on page 105)

SEVERINE : *Me? But, I . . . I was going to . . .*

She stops, at a loss. The PROFESSOR makes a little gesture towards her with his hand and adds in a very sharp voice :

PROFESSOR : *Get dressed again, please.*

Then he shuts himself up in the bathroom again. SEVERINE, puzzled, puts the dressing gown back on and does it up. A few seconds later, we hear someone knocking timidly at the bathroom door. SEVERINE hesitates a moment and then she replies :

SEVERINE : *Come in.*

The door opens and the PROFESSOR appears. He is dressed as a servant in a stately home: striped waistcoat, wing collar, black tie and black trousers. In his hand he is holding the leather scourge. SEVERINE turns and looks at him, very surprised. Looking extremely respectful and timid, as though he has done something wrong, the PROFESSOR advances two or three steps into the Pink Room towards SEVERINE, and asks humbly:

PROFESSOR: *Madame la Marquise called for me?*

SEVERINE uncertainly: *Yes* . . .

The PROFESSOR comes round in front of SEVERINE and continues, looking fixedly at her:

PROFESSOR: *Madame la Marquise isn't satisfied with my services?*

SEVERINE falters and, in spite of the lessons which CHARLOTTE has given her, she stammers a little:

SEVERINE: *Well, I . . . No, quite right, no . . .*

These hesitations seriously upset the PROFESSOR. He abandons his modest, servile attitude and again becomes a man used to having authority. Camera pans with him as he goes rapidly to the door which gives onto the corridor, opens it and calls:

PROFESSOR: *Madame Anaïs!*

ANAIS answers from outside (she wasn't far away).

ANAIS off: *Yes, here I am.*

The PROFESSOR turns to SEVERINE and says contemptuously:

PROFESSOR: *You belong in the kitchen . . . mademoiselle.*

ANAIS appears in the doorway. Very severely, the PROFESSOR points at SEVERINE and says:

PROFESSOR: *Take her away. She's no good. Bring Charlotte here, quick!*

ANAIS: *Immediately.* Camera pans as she moves across to SEVERINE and leads her away by the arm, saying: *Come on, you.*

SEVERINE goes out of the room with ANAIS, while the discontented PROFESSOR goes back into the bathroom and shuts himself in.

Medium shot of the corridor. Camera tracks in, tilting

up, as the two women come towards us. ANAIS calls
CHARLOTTE, who replies from some way away.

ANAIS : *Charlotte, go to the Professor straight away.*

CHARLOTTE : *One second, madame, I'm just getting undressed.*

ANAIS pushes SEVERINE towards the little sitting room
between the two bedrooms. ANAIS is angry.

ANAIS to SEVERINE : *Go in here . . . You don't have to be
a genius . . .*

They both go into the little sitting room.

Medium close-up of SEVERINE coming into the little
sitting room. Situated between the Blue Room and the
Pink Room, it is really a reception room. It is here that
clients are received and where they wait, if the need
arises. For the time being, there is no one there. ANAIS
comes into shot, moves a small painting on the wall and
uncovers a spyhole through which it is possible to see
into the Pink Room without being seen. (Still on page 105)

ANAIS beckoning to SEVERINE : *Put yourself here. Watch
carefully how Charlotte does it. And for goodness sake don't
make any noise.*

Camera tracks in as SEVERINE stands and looks, in back
view. ANAIS goes out, leaving her alone.

In the Pink Room, which SEVERINE has just left, the
same scene begins again, but this time with CHARLOTTE.
Seen in medium shot, CHARLOTTE comes in through the
door. Camera tracks out in front of her as she walks
across to the bed. The PROFESSOR knocks timidly on the
bathroom door and CHARLOTTE, putting her hands on
her hips, says in an imperious voice :

CHARLOTTE : *Come in!*

Camera pans left, losing CHARLOTTE, as the PROFESSOR
comes in, wearing the same clothes, with the air of one
who is looking forward to his impending punishment.

PROFESSOR : *Madame la Marquise called for me?*

CHARLOTTE severe, off : *Yes, Victor.*

Camera pans to include CHARLOTTE as he comes round
behind her.

PROFESSOR anxious : *Madame la Marquise isn't satisfied with
my services?*

94

CHARLOTTE : *Victor, you make stupid mistakes all the time!*
She goes off.
PROFESSOR : *You're right . . . You're quite right, I admit
it . . .*
    Camera pans with him as he advances slowly towards
    CHARLOTTE. He says pitifully :
PROFESSOR : *But Madame la Marquise is so good, so kind
. . . and so very beautiful!*
CHARLOTTE : *Insolent wretch!*
    She walks round behind him and runs her finger along
    the top of the bed-board.
CHARLOTTE : *Just look at that, you must be blind. You see
that . . . There's dust everywhere . . .* Pointing : *And there,
look, look . . .*
    As she points, the PROFESSOR beats at the places she
    indicates with the leather scourge as if it were a duster.
    (Still on page 105)
    Close-up of the two of them. The PROFESSOR thrusts his
    face towards CHARLOTTE.
PROFESSOR : *I've broken a vase . . .*
    Medium close-up of the two of them. CHARLOTTE grips
    him by the arm.
CHARLOTTE : *A vase! I've just about had enough! This time,
Victor, you're fired.*
    She thrusts him away with an angry gesture. A panic-
    stricken look appears in the PROFESSOR's eyes. Camera
    pans as he pursues her across the room.
PROFESSOR : *No! No! I beg of you, no! Please, Madame la
Marquise, keep me!*
    She sits on the bed. He falls on his knees in front of her,
    with tears in his eyes, begging :
PROFESSOR : *Yes, please keep me! Give me another chance!
I shall be careful, I swear, very careful.*
    Reverse angle medium close-up of the two of them, the
    PROFESSOR facing camera. CHARLOTTE grabs the leather
    scourge from him and raises it threateningly. Suddenly,
    no longer acting, he says in his normal authoritarian
    voice :
PROFESSOR : *Not yet, Charlotte. Not yet. Give me that.* He

grabs it from her.

CHARLOTTE : *Oh, sorry.*

Immediately the PROFESSOR becomes the servant again and starts his lamentations once more.

PROFESSOR taking off his glasses : *Madame la Marquise can punish me, if she likes. Beat me even!* He hands CHARLOTTE the leather scourge and places both hands on her knees. *Trample on me, and crush me! But please don't throw me out!*

He pushes back CHARLOTTE's négligée and strokes her thighs. CHARLOTTE slaps the PROFESSOR's hand sharply.

CHARLOTTE : *What are you doing, you old pig?*

PROFESSOR : *Nothing, I wasn't doing anything . . . I'm keeping my distance, alas! Ah! I shouldn't say it! It's a secret! Madame la Marquise . . .* He leans his hands again on CHARLOTTE's knees . . . *I love you!*

CHARLOTTE : *What?*

She pushes him back by kicking him in the face. The PROFESSOR loses hold and falls backwards onto the floor. Camera pans with him as he crawls round the end of the bed on all fours, repeating :

PROFESSOR : *I love you. And now that I have told you that I love you . . .* (Still on page 105)

He rolls over on his back and CHARLOTTE's legs are seen as she hurries round him brandishing the leather scourge. The PROFESSOR, in his normal voice but out of breath, says to her :

PROFESSOR : *Now. Walk over me! Go on!*

High angle medium close-up of the PROFESSOR lying on the floor with CHARLOTTE's feet just next to him.

PROFESSOR : *Spit on me, trample on my face!*

CHARLOTTE climbs on his chest, then tramples on his face with her slippered feet. (Still on page 105)

CHARLOTTE : *You dirty old man! . . . You old pig! . . . I'll teach you a lesson!*

Medium close-up of SEVERINE standing at the secret spy-hole. She turns away as if disgusted but then moves back again and peers through the hole, obviously fascinated in spite of herself. (Still on page 105)

PROFESSOR off: *But I tell you . . . But I tell you that I love you! Harder, Madame la Marquise . . . hit me harder . . .*
We hear the sound of CHARLOTTE beating him with the leather scourge in the next room. The door opens offscreen and ANAIS comes in and says:

ANAIS: *Come on, there's someone waiting.*
SEVERINE leaves the spyhole with apparent regret and comes towards camera.

ANAIS: *Well, did you see? What do you think of it?*
SEVERINE: *How can anyone get so low . . . You must be used to it . . . But it disgusts me.*
ANAIS looks at her enigmatically, thinking no doubt that SEVERINE does not see what sort of person she is herself. Then she goes off and SEVERINE follows her.

A bulky ASIATIC has just arrived and is standing with MATHILDE in the entrance hall. The man opens a small Japanese lacquered box which he is holding. (We do not see the contents.) He shows it to MATHILDE. A curious humming noise comes from inside the box. He looks at her interrogatively. (Still on page 106) MATHILDE replies in tones of considerable disgust:

MATHILDE: *No thank you, monsieur. Not for me.*
Camera pans left as she goes off while the ASIATIC closes the box with a shrug. ANAIS and SEVERINE come into view from the left and camera pans back again as they go up to the ASIATIC. ANAIS introduces SEVERINE, asking him:

ANAIS: *What about this one? Will she do?*
SEVERINE reaches up, puts an arm round his neck and kisses him. The ASIATIC looks at SEVERINE, says something in an Eastern language, then pulls a small white card of the Diner's Club variety out of his pocket. He holds it out to ANAIS.

ANAIS: *What's this?*
She takes the card and examines it, then says in terrible English:

ANAIS reading the card: *Credit Card . . . Geishas' Club.*
She gives it back to the ASIATIC and says loudly, trying to make him understand with gestures:

ANAIS: *No, no . . . It's no good here . . .* Rubbing her thumb and forefinger together: *Cash!*

The man takes his card back. He nods, understanding, says something and pulls out some banknotes. ANAIS takes two and hands the rest back, saying to SEVERINE:

ANAIS: *All right. Go ahead.*

The ASIATIC takes SEVERINE, who kisses him. Holding her round the waist, he comes with her towards us. (Still on page 106) We follow them as they go off down the corridor to one of the bedrooms. He pauses several times to kiss her on the neck. In contrast to her previous manner, SEVERINE seems to be looking forward with enthusiasm to her work.

Medium shot inside the Blue Room. SEVERINE enters, followed by the ASIATIC, who is still clutching his lacquered box. He puts the box down on a chest of drawers, then takes off his hat and coat and hangs them up. Then he advances towards SEVERINE, taking off his jacket, and picks up the box, releasing a spate of incomprehensible words. Camera pans to follow his movements. He opens the box and hands it to SEVERINE. The same curious humming sound comes from it as before. She looks down into the box and then up at the ASIATIC, rather alarmed. (Still on page 106) The ASIATIC gestures reassuringly and says in pidgin French:

ASIATIC: *Not to fear . . . Not to fear.*

Then he continues to talk to her in his own language, undressing as he does so. SEVERINE puts down the box and starts to take off her brassière. The ASIATIC objects volubly and points to her briefs, indicating that she should remove only them.

Medium close-up of the two of them from the waist up. The ASIATIC has now taken his shirt off, revealing an impressively muscled body. SEVERINE takes off her briefs and hands them to the ASIATIC, who has stretched out a hand. He inspects the briefs, still chattering away, then raises his arms. SEVERINE strokes his shoulder appreciatively. In his left hand he is holding a little bell, which he shakes.

Close-up of the ASIATIC's face. Camera pans across to his left hand as he shakes the bell, ringing it and talking at the same time. (Still on page 106) SEVERINE is watching him intrigued. She breaks into a smile and suddenly draws the ASIATIC towards her, flinging her arms round his neck.

Medium close-up of PALLAS, the maidservant, just inside the front door at ANAIS's. She has just let in a little girl aged about twelve. This is CATHERINE, PALLAS's daughter; she has just returned from school and is carrying a brief-case. (Still on page 106)

PALLAS : *Have you been working hard?*

CATHERINE : *Yes, Mummy.*

PALLAS : *Have you been a good girl?*

CATHERINE : *Yes, Mummy.*

PALLAS : *Go and say hello to your godmother. Show your lessons to her.*

Camera pans with the little girl as PALLAS propels her into the living room. ANAIS, who is with MATHILDE in the living room, sees her goddaughter and comes forward to kiss her on the cheek.

ANAIS : *Hello, Cathy!*

CATHERINE : *Hello!*

ANAIS : *How are you getting on? Show me your report card . . .*

CATHERINE opens her brief-case. ANAIS takes out the report card and starts to read it.

[ANAIS : *Eight out of ten in history, nine in recitation . . . That's good . . .* Frowning : *' Passable ' in behaviour?*

PALLAS : *She's a bit careless.*

ANAIS indulgent : *Well . . . we must be careful . . .* Giving her a packet of sweets : *There you are.*

CATHERINE : *Thank you, Godmother.*]*

MATHILDE, who is sitting at the table in the background, calls her and CATHERINE goes over and kisses her.

---

* This section of dialogue is not heard in the film. However, it will be noted that a condensed version of Anaïs's comments appears a little later in this scene.

MATHILDE : *Aren't you going to say hello to me?** 
CATHERINE : *Hello, Madame Mathilde.* 
MATHILDE : *Hello, you. Shall we go to the fair on Sunday?* 
CATHERINE : *Oh yes!* 
MATHILDE : *Would you like that?* 
CATHERINE : *Yes!* 

ANAIS, who has been standing reading the report card in the foreground, beckons her over and says : 
ANAIS : *Seven in history, nine in recitation . . . That's good.* 
She puts her arm round CATHERINE. 
Long shot of the corridor. Camera tracks out as CHARLOTTE pokes her head out of the Pink Room at the end. 
CHARLOTTE shouting : *Madame Anaïs! Madame Anaïs!* 
PALLAS appears from a doorway in the foreground. 
ANAIS off : *What?* 
CHARLOTTE : *Now the Professor wants an inkpot.* 
ANAIS appears in back view in the foreground. 
ANAIS : *What's going on?* 
CHARLOTTE : *He wants an inkpot.* 
ANAIS shrugging : *An inkpot? I haven't got one.* She goes off. 
A longer shot of the corridor. The ASIATIC comes out of the Blue Room and strides towards camera, carrying his little box and jingling his bell. As he reaches the entrance hall, CATHERINE appears on her way out. He seizes her by the arm and starts to pet her, chattering away in his own language. PALLAS appears and grabs her daughter indignantly by the other arm. Camera pans left as, still holding her daughter, she goes across and opens the front door. The ASIATIC goes out, bowing and taking off his hat. PALLAS half-closes the door again and says to her daughter : 
PALLAS : *Now go upstairs quickly. Go and do your homework.* 
CATHERINE obediently kisses her on the cheek. 
CATHERINE : *Yes, Mummy.* 

The little girl goes out and up the stairs while PALLAS follows her onto the landing and peers downwards. The ASIATIC's bell can still be heard tinkling faintly as he 

---

\* In the original script Catherine has this conversation with Charlotte, who comes in having at last finished with the Professor.

goes on his way.

Medium shot of the Blue Room. SEVERINE is sprawled face downwards on the bed, completely motionless. PALLAS walks across the room carrying a towel and lights the bedside lamp, which has been knocked over; then she comes slowly towards the bed and draws the crumpled sheet over SEVERINE's naked behind.

Low angle medium shot of the bed with SEVERINE lying across it in the foreground. PALLAS leans over her and says quietly, thinking that SEVERINE is dejected, exhausted :

PALLAS : *That man frightens me too . . . it really must be hard sometimes . . .*

She moves away and camera tracks in on SEVERINE, who raises her head towards PALLAS. Her cheeks are flushed, she looks happy and calm. She replies languidly :

SEVERINE : *What do you know about it, Pallas?*

[Exterior shot of a café, daytime. SEVERINE is sitting alone on the terrace of the café where we have already seen her during the first sequence. She looks around her, apparently happy, then suddenly, astonished, she looks towards the street in the front of the café terrace. The sound of bells can be heard.]*

Long shot of the Bois de Boulogne as seen from the terrace of an open-air café. The sound of bells can be heard off. Camera pans through 180° as the same landau as we have already seen drives up and comes to a halt. It is drawn by the same two horses and driven by the same COACHMAN in livery. The same FOOTMAN is sitting beside the COACHMAN, his arms crossed, impassive. This time, however, it is not PIERRE who is sitting in the carriage, but an oldish man we do not know. This man gets out of the landau, comes towards the café terrace and starts to move forward among the tables, looking around him. Dressed in dark clothes, he is wearing a hat and gloves,

---

* This section was not seen in the version screened. In the original script, the following scenes with the Duke do not occur until after the fantasy scene with Husson in the bar (see page 117 and footnote).

carrying a cane and has a monocle in one eye. Very smart, very distinguished, he has a lot of presence. Camera pans with him as he moves past SEVERINE, who is seated alone with her back to camera. He notices her, stops and removes his hat. He asks with the greatest courtesy, indicating a vacant chair:

DUKE : *May I, mademoiselle?* (Still on page 107)

SEVERINE : *Please do.*

DUKE : *Thank you.*

Reverse angle medium close-up of SEVERINE. The DUKE sits down beside her, and asks:

DUKE : *Mademoiselle . . . or madame?*

SEVERINE with a faint smile : *Mademoiselle.*

DUKE apparently satisfied : *Perfect . . .* He removes his monocle. *And . . . what is your name?*

SEVERINE : *Belle de Jour.*

DUKE : *Charming. I once had a cat called Belle de l'Ombre.*

Camera tracks in on the DUKE, losing SEVERINE.

DUKE : *Do you come here often?*

SEVERINE off : *Every day in my thoughts . . .*

Taking off his gloves, the DUKE starts to look around him, talking about nothing in particular.

DUKE : *What a lovely morning . . .*

SEVERINE : *Yes, it is.*

DUKE : *I like nothing better than the autumn sun . . . The black sun!* He looks at SEVERINE and camera pans across, losing him. (Still on page 107)

SEVERINE in puzzled tones, looking up at the sky : *The black sun?*

[With his cane he gestures towards their surroundings.

DUKE : *The world changes so much . . . Do you know, when my grandfather was a young man, this cross-roads was still a place where you could easily have your throat cut.*

SEVERINE politely : *Ah?*]*

DUKE off : *I think you're very elegant.*

SEVERINE turning towards him : *Thank you.*

DUKE off : *Do you like money?*

---

* This piece of dialogue does not occur in the film.

Severine looks down; her face hardens.

Severine murmuring : *Yes.*

Duke off : *I'll give you a lot if you'll come home with me* . . .

Severine looking across at him, surprised : *Home with you?*

Camera pans across to the Duke who, although he seems to know very well with whom he is dealing, is afraid of not making himself understood.

Duke : *Don't get me wrong . . . It's for a kind of religious ceremony — a very moving one — which is very dear to me* . . . He looks across at her and smiles briefly, then continues : *You see . . . I'm a man of another era . . . one in which people still had a feeling for death.* He puts his hand in his pocket. *If you agree to come, you'll make me a very happy man.* Camera pans across to Severine, who takes a sip of her drink as he continues off : *You are just the girl I am looking for . . . I live an hour away from Paris.*

Camera pans and tracks out to include the two of them as he hands her a visiting card. Severine takes the card and examines it while the Duke continues :

Duke : *I will meet you at the station.*

Medium close-up of the two horses drawing the landau as they stand in front of the café. Camera moves up to show the Coachman and the Footman, sitting impassively in their places.

High angle medium shot, panning with the landau as, with a jingle of harness, it moves up a carriage drive leading to a large red brick château in the country.* In it are seated Severine and the Duke, who is casually dressed. (Still on page 107)

A wood fire is blazing in the fireplace inside the Duke's boudoir. (Still on page 107) Camera pans left to an armchair as a man dressed in black approaches (we do not see his face), and lays Severine's dress and underwear down on the chair. He picks up a flowing

---

* In the original script, the Duke's house is not in the country, but is described as : ' an old town house in Paris (it could be one of those in the Marais district, around the Place des Vosges).' Also in the original script the Duke takes Séverine straight there in the landau.

black lace veil attached to a crown of white flowers. Camera tilts up to show his face. He is a character we have not seen before, the DUKE'S BUTLER, dressed in the appropriate uniform, but wearing dark glasses. (Still on page 107) He walks across the room to where SEVERINE is standing naked with her back to us beyond a large arrangement of gladioli.

BUTLER : *Here, put this on, please.*

He helps her to fix the veil on her hair. He seems very pleasant and respectful to SEVERINE.

*[In a nearby room, a PRIEST'S voice can be heard intoning a prayer of the mass. The BUTLER discreetly opens a door and looks into the next room.

This room turns out to be the chapel. In the centre of it is a catafalque, covered with a black sheet ornamented with silver. It is surrounded by burning candles. A PRIEST, assisted by a CHOIRBOY, is saying the Requiem Mass, which is just coming to an end. Turning round, he says :

PRIEST : *Ite missa est . . .*

DUKE and CHOIRBOY : *Deo gratias . . .*

The DUKE is kneeling on a prayer-stool, his head in his hands. He is the only person attending the mass.

Inside the DUKE'S boudoir, the BUTLER comes back towards SEVERINE and says to her :

BUTLER : *It'll soon be over. Are you ready?*]

SEVERINE : *But what's it all about?*

The BUTLER, still courteous, replies, while straightening the folds in the lace veil. He turns her round to face him.

BUTLER : *Don't be alarmed. You know, those who've been before you wouldn't ask for anything better than to come again . . . But the Duke is very strict on that point . . .*

He walks across the room and camera pans as SEVERINE follows him.

BUTLER standing at the door : *If you would be so good as to follow me.* (Still on page 107)

She precedes him through the door, then he leads her

---

* This following section in square brackets, and the succeeding one in the same scene, reflect the fact that all references to a religious service were cut by the French Censor.

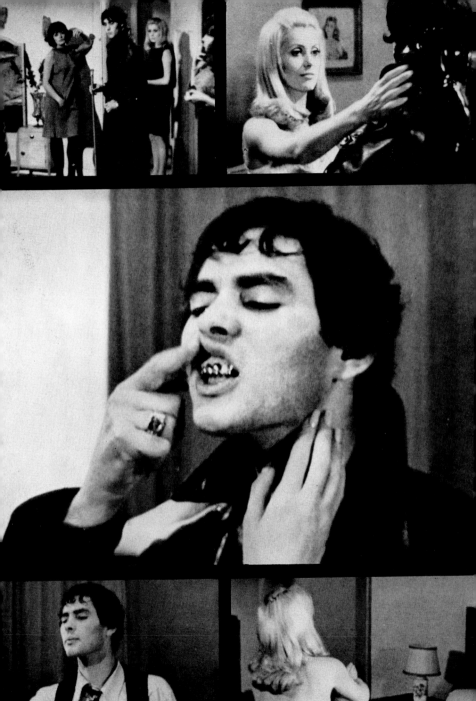

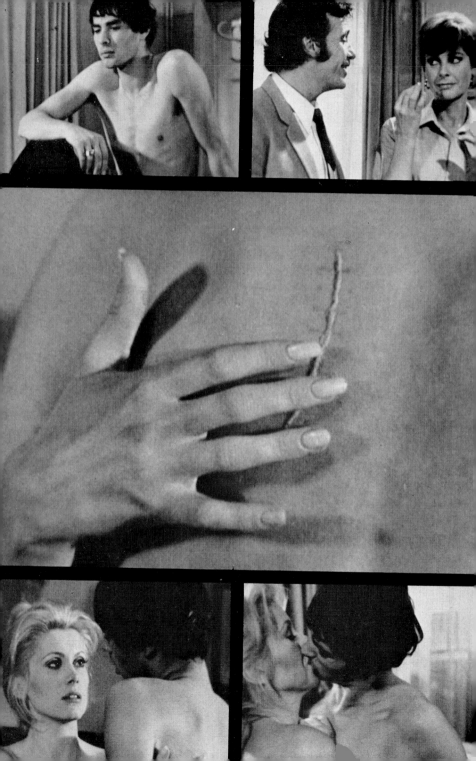

down the corridor away from camera.

BUTLER : *This way, please.* Sounds of a thunderstorm off.

Reverse angle shot. Camera pans with SEVERINE as she follows the BUTLER through another room and off round the corner.

BUTLER pausing in the doorway : *This way!*

[Hearing the signal that mass has finished in the next room, he says :

BUTLER : *I think it's time now.*

He looks through the half-open door again and signals to SEVERINE.

BUTLER : *Yes. Come along.*

Both of them go into the chapel.

The chapel is empty. The BUTLER removes the catafalque and helps SEVERINE to lie down in the coffin. At the same time, he gives her his final instructions :

BUTLER : *There . . . The main thing is not to move. Put your hands together, close your eyes . . . Breathe as weakly as possible . . . I'll leave you now . . .*

He moves away, leaving SEVERINE alone in the chapel, after arranging the folds of the lace veil around her.

SEVERINE, her eyes closed, hands together, waits for a few moments.]

Low angle shot of the DUKE as he enters the chapel in evening dress, carrying a camera on a tripod and a bunch of lilies. (Still on page 107) He puts down the tripod and walks across to the catafalque, which appears in the foreground. SEVERINE is lying in it with her eyes closed and her hands crossed on her breast as if dead. There is a lighted candle on each corner. The DUKE gazes down at SEVERINE, removes his monocle and lays his bunch of lilies on her body. (Still on page 107)

DUKE : *I brought you some lilies . . . you loved them so much . . .* He seems very moved. A tear trickles down his cheek. *How beautiful you are . . . Your skin is even whiter . . .* He lifts a lock of SEVERINE's hair with his hand. *Your hair is even softer . . .*

Medium close-up of the DUKE looking down at the catafalque. Camera pans with him as he moves round to the other side.

DUKE : *My beloved daughter* . . .

Camera tilts down to include SEVERINE lying apparently lifeless in the coffin as the DUKE leans over her and touches her face gently. (Still on page 108)

DUKE : *Only yesterday, we played together. We laughed and sang . . . Now you just lie there and say nothing . . . You don't move* . . . Bowing his head, as though shaken by some obscure remorse : *I hope you have forgiven me . . . It wasn't my fault . . . I loved you too much* . . .

He raises his head as there is a loud knock on the door.

Medium shot of the BUTLER standing outside the door.

BUTLER : *Monsieur le Duc, shall I let the cats in?*

Resume on the DUKE. He looks up angrily and shouts :

DUKE : *Go to hell with your cats* . . . He pauses, drops his voice and says : *We're alone, the doors are closed* . . . He laughs, looking down at SEVERINE. Then his expression suddenly becomes grim. *Now your eyes will never open again. Your limbs are stiff and your heart is being eaten by worms . . . And this heady odour of dead flowers* . . .

His voice gets fainter and fainter as he repeats the last phrase and finally it is impossible to hear what he is saying. His lips continue moving for a short time; he looks distracted. Then he stiffens. His look becomes glazed. He stares fixedly at SEVERINE's face for several seconds. Suddenly he bends down and disappears behind the catafalque. There is a loud peal of thunder.

Close-up of SEVERINE lying in the coffin, which starts to rock slightly as the thunder continues. SEVERINE opens her eyes, pauses for a moment with a surprised look on her face and sits up slowly, without making the slightest noise. She manages to lean over the edge of the coffin. We do not see what she sees, but only her face. She seems to find it very interesting, but rather disgusting at the same time. (Still on page 108)

Shot of the hallway in the DUKE's house. A moment later, the BUTLER comes in; camera pans left as he crosses the room and finds SEVERINE standing, apparently waiting for something. The BUTLER's attitude has totally

114

changed. In a very violent, very scornful tone, he says to SEVERINE:

BUTLER: *Haven't you gone yet? What are you waiting for?*

We hear the noise of rain outside and SEVERINE, surprised by the BUTLER's attitude, says, as though she were looking for an excuse:

SEVERINE: *But . . . it's raining and . . .*

BUTLER: *And what?*

He takes her by the arm and drags her vigorously towards the open door, shouting:

BUTLER: *Just get the hell out of here, will you?*

With a brutal push, he thrusts her out into the pouring rain and hurls her coat, which he has picked up, after her. He slams the glass door shut and stands watching SEVERINE as she slings the coat round her shoulders, looking back at him fearfully. She hurries off into the pouring rain.

The scene changes to the interior of PIERRE's and SEVERINE's bedroom. It is night. Camera pans from SEVERINE's empty bed to show PIERRE, sitting up in his bed, reading some notes by the light of his bedside lamp before going to sleep. The noise of bottles being knocked against each other can be heard in the bathroom, off. PIERRE throws down the notes and says:

PIERRE: *Have you nearly finished?*

SEVERINE off: *I'm coming.*

Medium shot of the door of the bedroom. SEVERINE, in her nightdress, comes through and turns the bathroom light out. (Still on page 109) Pan as she goes towards her bed, which is turned back. She sits on the bed and looks eagerly at PIERRE.

SEVERINE: *Shall I stay with you?*

She turns out the bedside lamp and goes towards him. Camera tracks out to show his bed in the foreground. She gets in and snuggles down beside him. PIERRE takes her in his arms. (Still on page 109)

PIERRE surprised: *I only wish you'd stay with me more often . . . of your own free will . . .*

115

SEVERINE : *I will, Pierre . . . Give me time . . .*

PIERRE : *I always get the feeling that I'm forcing something on you . . .*

    Close-up of their faces on the pillow.

SEVERINE : *Don't think that. I want more and more to be alone with you. You don't frighten me any more. I seem to be getting to understand you better, getting closer to you . . . I love you more every day, you know . . .*

    PIERRE draws her close to him, tenderly. They kiss.


    Medium shot of the entrance hall in SEVERINE'S flat. It is daytime. The MAID appears from the background and opens the front door. HUSSON enters and says :

HUSSON : *Good morning, mademoiselle. Is Madame at home?*

MAID : *Whom shall I say?*

HUSSON : *Monsieur Husson.* (Still on page 109)

    She goes off into the drawing room and camera tracks in on HUSSON as he starts to take off his scarf and coat.*

MAID to SEVERINE off : *Monsieur Husson would like to see you, madame . . .*

SEVERINE off : *Tell him I'm not in.*

    Hearing this exchange, HUSSON pauses with his coat half off and puts it back on again. (Still on page 109) He is just putting on his scarf as the MAID reappears.

HUSSON : *Goodbye, mademoiselle. Thank you.*

    He picks up his hat and goes out. The MAID shuts the door behind him.

    Medium close-up of SEVERINE sitting on the sofa in the drawing room reading a magazine. Seen through the open doorway in the background, the MAID closes the front door and then goes off. SEVERINE glances round as she does so, then throws down her magazine and leans her head on her hand. She looks disturbed and pensive. She daydreams. (Stills on page 109)

    Suddenly the interior of the bar at the winter sports

---

* In the original script, this sequence starts with Séverine in the drawing room, getting ready to go out. The maid comes in with the news of Husson's arrival, then we see Husson who, having overheard their conversation, leaves without waiting for the maid to return.

resort, which we have already seen, reappears. We see SEVERINE and HUSSON in medium close-up gazing into each other's eyes. HUSSON speaks to SEVERINE :

HUSSON : *You're very attractive, Séverine* . . . Carrying on in a casual tone : *But, let's be frank: I want to write you a letter.*

SEVERINE her eyes lighting up : *I'd like that.*

HUSSON still gazing at her : *But would you let me?* He looks around. *There are too many people here* . . .

SEVERINE : *So much the better!*

HUSSON leans towards her and, looking her straight in the eyes, says :

HUSSON : *I've absolutely got to give you the receipt.*

SEVERINE : *I'm relying on it.*

Camera tracks back to show RENEE and PIERRE seated at the same table in the background. HUSSON seizes a bottle by the neck and breaks it on the table with a violent blow.

HUSSON : *With this?*

SEVERINE : *Yes.*

They both disappear under the table.* (Stills on page 109)

PIERRE shifts into SEVERINE'S seat and says to RENEE :

PIERRE : *What are they doing?*

RENEE glances under the table, then with exaggerated nonchalance says :

RENEE : *Oh, nothing . . . Fooling around . . . Have a look!*

PIERRE looking uncomfortable : *No, no. You tell me.*

The table begins to rock slightly.

RENEE looking under the table again : *He's taking out a little envelope* . . .

PIERRE : *And then* . . . *?*

RENEE with innocent surprise : *No . . . It's a little packet of lily seeds.*

PIERRE looks uncomfortable and says :

PIERRE : *Oh yes. I see.*

---

* In the original script, the scene ends at this point and we return briefly to Séverine in the drawing room of her apartment. The scenes with the Duke then follow.

Long shot of the Champs-Elysées in the daytime. A young NEWSPAPER-SELLER walks along the pavement towards camera, shouting:

PAPER-SELLER: *' Herald Tribune '! ' New York Herald Tribune '! ' Herald Tribune '!* (Still on page 110)

A man buys a paper from him, then goes into a block of offices, camera panning with him. He is aged about fifty, very strong, with broad shoulders, wearing a beige raincoat and trilby. His rugged face can look either good-natured or threatening. His name is HIPPOLYTE.

Medium shot of the vestibule of the building. Hanging about just inside a row of glass doors, elaborately doing nothing, is a young man dressed in a long black leather overcoat and carrying a cane. He is tall and thin; he looks nervous and has a scar on his face. His name is MARCEL. He looks very sinister. A CASHIER dressed in a dark uniform and carrying a black document case comes through the glass doors, walking quickly. Camera pans left as MARCEL immediately starts to follow him past the staircase towards the lifts. The CASHIER stops by one of the lifts. He seems a little anxious and glances rapidly at MARCEL, who has stopped just opposite him. A lift door clangs on another floor.

Medium close-up of the CASHIER, with MARCEL in back view in the foreground. The CASHIER is visibly disturbed by this rather dubious-looking individual. He tucks the document case under his arm and camera tracks out in front of him, panning to lose MARCEL, as he goes over to one of the other lifts, where HIPPOLYTE is standing absorbed in the *New York Herald Tribune*. He glances at the CASHIER and folds his paper as the lift arrives. He opens the gates and steps in, in front of the CASHIER, asking him:

HIPPOLYTE: *What floor?*

CASHIER: *Fourth, please.*

He steps in after HIPPOLYTE and is about to shut the gates when MARCEL dashes up and into the lift.

MARCEL: *Excuse me.*

MARCEL slams the gates closed. A struggle ensues as the

lift moves off and we hear muffled shouting from the
CASHIER.

CASHIER: *Hey! What are you doing? Help! . . . Help! . . .*
The lift rises out of sight behind the wrought iron gates.
A shot of the lift shaft from another floor. Camera tilts
up as the lift moves past. More muffled shouting is heard
from inside. We catch a glimpse through the gates of the
men struggling.
A shot from inside the lift. The iron gates are seen in
silhouette as several floors shoot past outside.

HIPPOLYTE in a loud whisper: *Take it easy, mate . . .* To
MARCEL: *Hurry up . . . quick!*
Medium close-up of the lift gates on another floor. Camera
tilts up as the lift moves past inside.
Medium shot of the lift gates on another floor. The lift
arrives and HIPPOLYTE comes out, followed by MARCEL,
who is holding the CASHIER'S case. The doors clang shut
behind them. MARCEL tucks the case inside his overcoat.
They both look round furtively, and camera pans with
them as they go off down the ornamental staircase. Tilt
down to show the landing below. HIPPOLYTE halts, looks
over the banister and signals to MARCEL that all is clear.
They both hurry off. (Still on page 110)
Medium shot of the entrance to the building from the
Champs-Elysées. MARCEL comes out first, swinging his
cane, and walks off up the street. A few seconds later,
HIPPOLYTE comes out, swinging his rolled-up newspaper.
Camera pans as he goes off in the opposite direction.
Medium shot of HIPPOLYTE ringing the door bell outside
ANAIS'S flat. MARCEL appears in back view as ANAIS
opens the door. She does not seem too pleased to see
them.

ANAIS: *Hippolyte . . . What a surprise!*

HIPPOLYTE in a thick Spanish accent: *Hello, Anaïs. Can we
come in?*

ANAIS after a moment's hesitation: *Of course.*
She stands back and lets the two men in. Camera tracks
through the door after them.

ANAIS pointing down the corridor: *That way.*

119

Camera pans to show them from behind as they walk away down the corridor.

In the living room are the three girls. CHARLOTTE is sewing; SEVERINE is polishing her nails; MATHILDE, more curious, has got up. We first see her in medium close-up as she looks through the glass door into the entrance hall. Camera pans as she walks across to the table where the other two women are seated. (Still on page 110)

MATHILDE not very happy: *It's Hippolyte* . . .

CHARLOTTE jumping slightly: *The Murcian?*

MATHILDE: *Yes.*

This news seems to put CHARLOTTE in a bad temper.

CHARLOTTE: *I thought we'd got rid of him* . . .

MATHILDE standing in front of the table: *There are two of them* . . . *I don't know who the other one is.*

SEVERINE who is smoking a cigarette: *Who's Hippolyte?*

CHARLOTTE: *Wait and see. He's a funny sort of guy.*

Camera pans with MATHILDE as she moves, losing SEVERINE.

MATHILDE: *When he's got money, he throws it about* . . .

CHARLOTTE: *But when he's broke, he gets it for free* . . .

Camera pans across to the door as ANAIS looks in and says:

ANAIS: *Come here, girls! All three of you!*

They go out in single file.

High angle medium shot of the Pink Room, with MARCEL standing in the foreground. Camera pans as HIPPOLYTE crosses the room and sits on the bed. He grabs PALLAS by the arm as she passes carrying some linen.

HIPPOLYTE: *Hey! How's the little one? Okay?* . . .

PALLAS nervously: *Yes, monsieur.*

HIPPOLYTE: *Ready to be kissed yet?*

PALLAS quavering: *I don't know, monsieur. She has to finish at school.*

HIPPOLYTE: *Ah, splendid!* . . .

He thrusts a note at her. She pauses, then takes it without a word and goes off. Camera pans right as ANAIS comes in through the door, followed by the three girls.

Good-tempered and smiling, HIPPOLYTE sits on the bed, smoking a cigarette. He draws ANAIS to him and puts his arm round her waist while the three girls file in and stand facing him.

ANAIS : *You'll have nothing to complain about.*

SEVERINE : *Hello.*

MATHILDE : *Hello, Monsieur Hippolyte . . .*

CHARLOTTE : *Hello, Hippolyte . . .*

HIPPOLYTE looks at all three of them quite squarely, one after the other, then he says in Spanish :

HIPPOLYTE : *' Buen ganao '\* . . .*

ANAIS : *What does that mean?*

In reply HIPPOLYTE makes a vulgar gesture, jerking his thumb in the air and clicking his tongue. ANAIS nods comprehendingly. HIPPOLYTE looks at CHARLOTTE.

HIPPOLYTE : *Okay?*

CHARLOTTE : *Okay . . . and you?*

HIPPOLYTE : *I'm not complaining, thanks.*

Close-up of MATHILDE.

MATHILDE : *We haven't seen you for months, Monsieur Hippolyte.*

Camera pans to CHARLOTTE. The two women assume a commercial smile while speaking to him. They force themselves to be agreeable.

CHARLOTTE : *We missed you a lot.*

HIPPOLYTE rather incredulous, off : *Oh yes?*

CHARLOTTE : *Where have you been?*

Camera pans slowly to SEVERINE as HIPPOLYTE replies :

HIPPOLYTE off : *I've been away . . . To New York . . .* In English : *Business . . .*

SEVERINE tosses her head.

High angle medium shot of HIPPOLYTE still sitting on the end of the bed; ANAIS stands behind him with her arm round his neck. HIPPOLYTE is in an expansive mood and, since he has been rich for an hour, he is going to be generous. Turning towards ANAIS, he says :

HIPPOLYTE : *Put three bottles to chill. Good ones.*

---

\* Literally : ' fine cattle ' or ' livestock '.

ANAIS : *The very best.* She goes off.

HIPPOLYTE pats his knee in invitation to MATHILDE, who has been standing back to camera in the foreground. She goes and sits on his knee, while CHARLOTTE comes round behind him and leans on his shoulder. (Still on page 110)

HIPPOLYTE : *' De Paris al cielo! '\* The thing that you miss most abroad is champagne . . .* MATHILDE caresses his ear, smiling . . . *' y las francesitas cachondas como tu! '\*\**

HIPPOLYTE'S announcement seems to have made CHAR-LOTTE and MATHILDE relax, since it appears to mean that he has money. SEVERINE has come into view and is wandering around in the background, glancing at MAR-CEL off-screen. She now sits on the edge of a table as MARCEL appears and stands looking out of the window with his back to the others. HIPPOLYTE gestures in the direction of MARCEL, who has not yet taken part in the proceedings, and says to MATHILDE :

HIPPOLYTE : *I've brought you someone. He's a friend, so you've got to be kind to him.*

MATHILDE : *Of course, Monsieur Hippolyte.*

She kisses him while CHARLOTTE leans forward to watch. Medium close-up of MARCEL standing at the window. He seems much more shy than HIPPOLYTE with the women and has hitherto ignored their presence. He now turns round quickly towards the three women, without greeting them or saying anything else. Camera tracks out to include SEVERINE as his eyes fall on her. She looks at him. She seems impressed by this newcomer.

CHARLOTTE off : *Monsieur Hippolyte . . . When we're alone I'll tell you a new story. You'll like it.*

HIPPOLYTE : *You can keep it.*

CHARLOTTE : *Too bad for you.*

HIPPOLYTE : *' Vaca.'\*\*\**

During this conversation camera pans across to HIP-POLYTE with the two girls, cutting out MARCEL and SEVERINE.

---

\* ' From Paris to heaven.'
\*\* ' And sexy little French bits like you.'
\*\*\* ' Cow.'

HIPPOLYTE : *Get off. You're too heavy.*
MATHILDE indignantly : *What's up?*
He makes an impatient gesture. She gets up and goes off.
HIPPOLYTE addresses CHARLOTTE, who is still caressing
his ear :
HIPPOLYTE : . . . *And you're tickling me. You get out too.*
She sighs and goes off also. *Come here a bit, you, the new girl.*
Camera tilts up and pans left as he stands up and draws
SEVERINE towards him. MARCEL watches in the back-
ground.
HIPPOLYTE : *Well . . . now . . .*
He is about to take her in his arms when MARCEL
stretches out his cane and places it between them. They
both look at him. (Still on page 110)
MARCEL : *Leave her to me.* SEVERINE hurries out of shot.
Close-up of HIPPOLYTE. He puts his hands on his hips
and looks hard at MARCEL without speaking. Camera
tracks out to include MARCEL as HIPPOLYTE takes a step
towards him and says :
HIPPOLYTE : *Take her, kid, if you want her . . . Have a
good time. You should at your age . . .*
Camera pans as MARCEL passes in front of HIPPOLYTE
without a word. The three women are revealed : SEVERINE
standing in the open doorway, CHARLOTTE and MATHILDE
on either side. CHARLOTTE and MATHILDE look at the
two men with a certain amount of anxiety, as though
they had expected a confrontation between them. They
know that no one usually talks in that way to HIPPOLYTE.
(Still on page 111) MARCEL pauses, turns back towards
HIPPOLYTE and says :
MARCEL : *Thanks.* He pushes SEVERINE out through the door.
When they have gone out, camera tracks in on HIPPO-
LYTE as he goes up to MATHILDE and remarks :
HIPPOLYTE : *For less than that, I'd slit my father's throat.* He
raises his hand. *But friendship comes first. We're not going to
argue about ' una zorra '.*\*
Pan, losing MATHILDE, as HIPPOLYTE sits on the end of

---

\* Literally : ' A vixen.'

the bed again. CHARLOTTE comes up and puts her arm round his neck.

CHARLOTTE : *Your friend looks shy.*

HIPPOLYTE : *Shy isn't the word.*

Rapid pan to the doorway as ANAIS appears, a cigarette hanging from the corner of her mouth.

ANAIS very blasé : *The champagne's ready. Aren't you thirsty?* They all go out of the room. HIPPOLYTE, who is last, gives CHARLOTTE a hearty slap on the behind as she goes through the door.

[In the corridor, MARCEL walks in front, followed by SEVERINE. He opens the door of the Blue Room and goes in first. SEVERINE follows him obediently.

Inside the Blue Room : as soon as SEVERINE has come in, MARCEL closes the door with a kick and looks for a long time at this woman he does not know. During the whole scene he never stops talking to her and looking at her as though he utterly despised her. SEVERINE goes and lies on the bed, undoing the belt of her dressing gown. She waits. MARCEL remains near the door, his back against the wall.]*

Inside the Blue Room, MARCEL is seen in back view as he walks away from camera, slinging his boots over his shoulder. After a moment's silence he asks between his teeth :

MARCEL : *What's your name?*

SEVERINE off : *Belle de Jour . . .*

MARCEL : *And?*

SEVERINE off : *That's all.*

MARCEL nods his head, remains silent for a moment, then insists :

MARCEL : *Don't you trust me?* He comes across to her. Camera pans left with him. *I want to know your name.*

SEVERINE undressing : *Belle de Jour.*

Camera tracks in as he stands close to her.

MARCEL : *Why? . . . Aren't you here at night? What are you doing here?*

---

* This section was not seen in the version screened.

SEVERINE reaches up and takes his boots from him, changing the subject. (Still on page 111)

SEVERINE : *What nice boots.*

She throws them aside and puts her arms round him. They kiss. Suddenly she draws back and looks at him in surprise.

SEVERINE stroking his head : *What happened to your teeth?*

Reverse angle medium close-up of the two of them.

MARCEL almost proudly : *Knocked out all at once . . .*

Camera tracks in, cutting out SEVERINE, as he rolls back his lips to show his front teeth, which are all in gold. (Still on page 111)

MARCEL : *Does it bother you?*

SEVERINE off : *No . . .*

MARCEL : *Then make it fast.*

Camera pans across to show a coat-stand by the door as MARCEL starts to undress. (Still on page 111)

MARCEL : *How old are you?*

SEVERINE off : *Twenty-three.*

MARCEL : *Do you have a protector?*

SEVERINE off : *What does that mean?*

MARCEL : *Are you free or what?*

SEVERINE off : *No.*

MARCEL : *Make plenty of money? It's a good business?*

SEVERINE off : *Yes, but . . .*

MARCEL taking off his waistcoat : *Don't tell me any lies . . . Okay?*

As he finishes, cut to high angle medium close-up of SEVERINE sitting on the bed, naked, back to camera. She is just about to take off her stockings when MARCEL cuts in. (Still on page 111)

MARCEL off : *No, don't take off your stockings.*

She turns round, surprised.

Reverse angle medium close-up of MARCEL taking off his tie.

MARCEL : *A girl tried to strangle me once . . .*

Resume on SEVERINE. Camera tracks in as she pulls up her stockings again.

MARCEL off : *Poor kid.*

125

SEVERINE suddenly turns round and says:

SEVERINE: *With you it's free . . . if you like.*

Resume on MARCEL, about to take off his shirt. He turns to face SEVERINE.

MARCEL arrogantly: *Naturally! I know plenty of girls who would like to be in your place at this moment.* He starts to take off his shirt.

Medium shot with link on the motion as he takes off his shirt.

MARCEL: *You still won't tell me your name?* He starts to walk towards her. *Anyway, you don't talk too much. So much the better. I prefer that. Can't stand girls who chatter.*

Camera tilts down as he sits down on the bed facing SEVERINE, whose knees appear in the foreground. She is evidently lying down. He casts an appraising eye over her body and says:

MARCEL: *Not bad.*

He forces her knees down and looks more closely. (Still on page 112)

MARCEL with a faint smile: *A pity you've only got two of them. Let's have a look . . . Turn over . . .* He motions with his hand and we hear her move. *What's that little brown mark?*

SEVERINE: *A birthmark.*

MARCEL: *Oh shit . . . I can't stand that . . . Get dressed.*

He gets off the bed, goes across the room and picks up his shirt.

Medium shot of the living room at ANAIS's. Camera pans with MATHILDE as she crosses the room to the table where HIPPOLYTE and CHARLOTTE are standing. On the table are several glasses, a full champagne bottle in an ice-bucket and the opened one in a plastic pail. HIPPOLYTE puts his glass down and remarks:

HIPPOLYTE: *Not quite chilled enough . . . as usual.*

CHARLOTTE notices the headline of the *New York Herald Tribune*, which is sticking out of HIPPOLYTE's pocket. She pulls it out and unfolds it, then asks him, smiling and very surprised:

CHARLOTTE: *You read English now?*

HIPPOLYTE : *God forbid.*
CHARLOTTE : *Well, then . . .*
HIPPOLYTE : *What's it got to do with you?*
    ANAIS appears in the foreground and walks round the
    table carrying another champagne bottle in an ice-bucket.
CHARLOTTE reading from the newspaper and mispronouncing
the words : ' *Aberfan Inquiry Accused.*'
    HIPPOLYTE gets annoyed and grabs the newspaper from
    her.
HIPPOLYTE : *That's enough.*
    The women all laugh at her mispronunciation. HIPPO-
    LYTE taps one of the ice-buckets and says to CHARLOTTE :
HIPPOLYTE : *Take that into the bedroom. I'm coming.* CHAR-
LOTTE goes off. HIPPOLYTE continues to ANAIS, pointing to the
other bottle : *The other one's for Marcel.*
    Camera tracks in, losing MATHILDE, as ANAIS goes round
    the table towards HIPPOLYTE.
ANAIS : *Who is your friend?*
HIPPOLYTE very seriously : *He saved my life last year. I love
him like a son . . . A pause. If it hadn't been for that, you
don't think I'd have left him the blonde, do you? Where does
she come from?*
ANAIS looks non-committal and asks : *Who, Belle de Jour?*
HIPPOLYTE : *Yes. Is she much in demand?*
    ANAIS makes an expressive noise as if to say : ' And how.'
MATHILDE off : *She's the one they really come for  . . .* They
turn towards her.
    High angle medium close-up of MATHILDE as seen by
    them, seated, holding her champagne glass.
MATHILDE with a hint of sourness : *First of all she's got class
. . . and then . . .*
HIPPOLYTE : *What?* He turns to ANAIS. *Huh?*
    Reverse angle medium close-up of HIPPOLYTE and ANAIS.
    She says very simply to him :
ANAIS : *She's a pearl.*
HIPPOLYTE : *A pearl?*
    Looking at him archly, she makes the motion of thread-
    ing a pearl. She bursts out laughing, as does HIPPOLYTE.
    (Still on page 112) He gestures understandingly and says :

127

Hippolyte : ' *Una Perla.*' Anais nods.

[Hippolyte thinks for a moment, then he looks at Mathilde :

Hippolyte to Mathilde : *I'll bet no one's had you yet today?* Mathilde shakes her head, a little embarrassed. Hippolyte takes a thick wad of notes from his pocket (the notes which have been taken from the Cashier's case) and, turning slightly so as not to show them, he detaches one and gives it to Mathilde.

Hippolyte : *Here, take this.*

Mathilde : *Oh, thank you, Hippolyte.*

Hippolyte shortly : *You can thank me later.* He goes out.]*

High angle medium shot of Marcel's socks lying in the armchair in the Blue Room. Camera pans to show the rest of his clothes strewn about the floor and comes to rest on his boots. We hear him and Severine talking off.

Severine off : *I thought you wanted to go.*

Marcel off : *I'm glad I stayed . . . I don't mind telling you: I like you.*

Medium close-up of the two of them sitting on the bed, naked, Marcel back to camera. Severine holds out her hand in front of her.

Severine happy : *Look at my hand . . . It's still trembling . . .* Marcel leans forward and kisses her.

Close-up of his back. He has a large scar over his shoulder-blade. Severine's hand touches it. (Still on page 112)

Resume on medium close-up of the two of them.

Severine : *What's that you've got there?* (Still on page 112)

Marcel glancing back over his shoulder : *A button-hole.*

Severine : *A knife wound?*

Reverse angle medium close-up of the two of them from above, Marcel facing camera.

Marcel : *Could be . . .* Camera pans slightly as he leans back on his elbow and looks up at her, then continues : *What are you doing here?*

Severine : *Don't ask me anything.* She lies down.

Marcel : *I'd have liked to have you till tonight. But I can't.*

---

* This section was not seen in the version screened.

128

SEVERINE stroking his hair: *I like you too, Marcel. Will you come again?*

MARCEL: *Maybe* . . . He shrugs.

Not understanding this reply, SEVERINE timidly makes a suggestion:

SEVERINE: *If you've no money, I can* . . .

MARCEL: *Money?* He lifts her by the chin and shakes his head . . . *I've got plenty of that.*

[Touched to the quick, he jumps up, plunges his hand in one of his jacket pockets, takes out one of the wads of notes which he has stolen the same day and brandishes it in front of SEVERINE.

MARCEL: *Look* . . .

A pause. MARCEL puts the money back in his pocket.]*

He looks arrogantly at SEVERINE.

SEVERINE with her hand on his chest: *You frighten me.*

Camera pans slightly left as he leans forward and takes her in his arms, kissing her. We leave them entwined. (Still on page 112)

Long shot of an immense deserted beach in the south of France. It is a day in autumn or winter. The whole of the following scene is accompanied by the roar of waves. PIERRE appears in the foreground dressed warmly in a sheepskin coat. (Still on page 145) Camera pans and tracks with him as he walks to and fro and goes up to SEVERINE, who is seated on a dead tree-trunk. She also is warmly dressed in trousers and a fur-collared coat. They seem depressed and PIERRE says, looking at his wife:

PIERRE: *You know you're bored* . . .

SEVERINE: *No, I'm not bored* . . . *I just want to go back to Paris.*

PIERRE pauses a little way away from her. (Still on page 145)

PIERRE: *You know that you can tell me everything, absolutely everything* . . . *But you're hiding something from me* . . .

SEVERINE says nothing and glances at him. He comes

---

* This section does not appear in the film.

towards her.

PIERRE : *If you'd tell me what's bothering you, perhaps I could help you . . .*

SEVERINE : *Tell you what?*

PIERRE lowering his voice : *That you love someone, Séverine . . .*

SEVERINE : *Someone else?*

PIERRE : *Yes.*

She gets up and walks towards camera, her hands in her pockets.

SEVERINE : *You know that's impossible.*

Camera tracks out in front of her as she walks, followed a few paces behind by PIERRE.

PIERRE : *I asked you to come on this short holiday to see if there was anything holding you back in Paris . . . I was right, too, because you do want to go back. But with you there's always . . .* He hesitates as though he dare not continue . . . *this distance . . .* He comes up beside her as they continue to walk. *I've never felt you really close to me . . .*

SEVERINE turning away from him : *I'm sorry.* They stop.

PIERRE : *I suppose it's my fault.*

SEVERINE turning to face him : *And you think I can't love you, in spite of that?*

PIERRE : *That's what I think, yes . . .* SEVERINE goes off.

Medium close-up, tracking with SEVERINE as she walks.

SEVERINE'S VOICE over : *I don't know how to explain . . . There are so many things I want to understand . . . things about myself . . .* Tenderly : *What I feel for you has nothing to do with pleasure . . . It's much more than that . . . I don't expect you to believe me, but I've never felt so close to you . . .*

PIERRE comes up and takes her by the arm. She stops.

PIERRE : *Do you want to go back to Paris?*

SEVERINE turning to him : *Pierre, I'm telling you, it's not that I'm bored with you. Not for a moment. If you like, we'll stay another week . . .*

PIERRE flatly : *No, no. We'll go back tomorrow. In any case, I've got to get back.* They walk off.

Low angle medium shot of the two of them from behind. They walk away from camera, which tilts down to show their car standing on the beach in the distance. SEVERINE walks in front. PIERRE walks slowly, several yards behind.

The scene changes to a small bar somewhere near the Pigalle. It is usually filled with a rather shady clientèle, but for the moment it is quiet and almost empty.

Medium shot of the BARMAN and two customers who are about to leave. They say goodbye and camera pans to follow them to the door as the BARMAN says to MARCEL, who is evidently sitting somewhere off :

BARMAN : *Got problems, Monsieur Marcel?*

HIPPOLYTE off : *Well, I've seen plenty hooked, but never one like you.*

MARCEL sharply, off : *Shut up, will you?*

HIPPOLYTE off : *You behaved like an imbecile, not like a man.*

[MARCEL does not say anything. *A woman you hardly know . . . Has she cleared off? Let her go, there's ten more where she came from.*]*

At this point the couple go out and two rather sinister-looking men enter the bar. Camera pans with them as, without a word, they slowly walk across to HIPPOLYTE and MARCEL, who are seated at a table by the window. (Still on page 145) One of them sits down; the other, thin-faced and wearing a beige trench coat, greets HIPPOLYTE and stands over him. HIPPOLYTE looks at him without a word, then moves over to make room for him. He sits down.

[Without moving from the bar, the BARMAN asks them :

BARMAN : *And what for these gentlemen?*

THIN-FACED MAN : *Nothing. We're not staying.*]*

Camera tracks in. The relationship between the four men seems rather strained. They look at each other for a moment, then HIPPOLYTE says menacingly out of the corner of his mouth :

HIPPOLYTE : *We waited for you on Thursday.*

THIN-FACED MAN : *So what?*

HIPPOLYTE looking at him : *Next time we don't wait, okay?*

---

* This piece of dialogue does not occur in the film.

The Thin-faced Man nods his head to show that he has understood, and adds:

Thin-faced Man: *We nearly didn't come today.*

Hippolyte: *Oh yes?*

Thin-faced Man: *We've had enough of this game.* With a gesture towards Marcel. *We're getting fed up with you and that little jerk . . .*

Suddenly Marcel whips the top off his cane, which turns out to contain a dagger. He strikes at the Thin-faced Man. Hippolyte is even quicker. He stops Marcel and forces him down.

Hippolyte with a lot of authority: *Don't fight with these punks.*

Marcel regretfully puts his weapon back. Camera tracks in to medium close-up of Hippolyte and the Thin-faced Man as the Barman says to them from the bar:

Barman off: *Hey, if you want to settle things, go outside.*

Hippolyte to the Barman: *Shut your trap, you.*

Hippolyte now has the situation well in hand. He looks in silence for a moment at the Thin-faced Man and then he stretches out his open hand to him and says:

Hippolyte: *The snow. We know you've got it on you.* He clicks his fingers.

The Thin-faced Man hesitates a little, looks at his companion, then takes a small packet from inside his raincoat and hands it furtively to Hippolyte, who puts it straight in his jacket pocket and adds:

Hippolyte: *We're not keeping you.*

He relights the stub of the cigar he has been smoking. The two men get up and start to leave. Camera pans across to Marcel, who looks up at the Thin-faced Man off-screen, and says calmly:

Marcel: *I'll settle with you about the little jerk.*

Low angle medium close-up of the two men, who have paused on their way out.

Thin-faced Man equally calmly: *As you like.* They go out. Camera pans back to Hippolyte and Marcel. (Still on page 145) Marcel bangs the dagger back into the cane with the palm of his hand. Hippolyte begins to sing a Spanish love song in a quavering flamenco style. He glances ironically at MARCEL as he comes to the words: ' Tengo una novia morena ' (' I have a brunette girlfriend '). MARCEL smiles faintly and shakes his head. HIPPOLYTE looks at the brandy bottle in front of him, finds it is empty and calls to the waiter in Spanish. MARCEL, who has been sitting nervously, leans over and takes HIPPOLYTE by the wrist, looking at his watch. He gets up with a theatrical gesture. Camera tilts with him.

HIPPOLYTE : *Where are you going?*

MARCEL : *To telephone.*

HIPPOLYTE : *Again!*

MARCEL does not reply and the BARMAN arrives with another bottle. Camera pans with MARCEL as he goes towards a telephone on the bar counter. While he dials the number he wants, we hear HIPPOLYTE and the BARMAN talking.

HIPPOLYTE off : *What a drag, these broads . . .*

BARMAN off : *You can say that again . . . He's hooked?* *

HIPPOLYTE off : *It's already cost him a lot. But that's always been his trouble. I can't do a thing about it.*

MARCEL gets his number and speaks in a low voice :

MARCEL : *Hello, Anaïs? It's Marcel . . . Any news? . . .*

We do not hear ANAIS's reply, but MARCEL's face lights up. He feverishly grabs the second ear-piece and clamps it to his other ear.

MARCEL : *Since when? It's true?* He listens for a moment. *I'm on my way.*

He hangs up and flourishes his cane with a gleeful exclamation (Still on page 145), then goes off.

In ANAIS's living room, SEVERINE is alone with MATHILDE. SEVERINE is reading a book, while MATHILDE is doing a crossword puzzle, with some difficulty. At first we see only her arms and the newspaper which has the puzzle in it lying on the table. She gets stuck on a word and reads out the clue.

---

* In the original script, Hippolyte replies to this : ' Yes, and when it gets hold of him he doesn't know what he's doing any more. He goes mad.'

MATHILDE: *'He carried his father on his back', in four letters, the second is an N.*

As she speaks, camera tilts up and tracks out to show the whole table with SEVERINE seated reading her book. SEVERINE interrupts her without looking up from the book:

SEVERINE: *'Enée'.\* With an E at the end.*

MATHILDE writing: *Oh yes, of course. It often comes up in crosswords.*

[At the beginning of this short dialogue, we have heard the front door bell ring.]\*\* ANAIS comes in through the door in the background and says to SEVERINE:

ANAIS: *Belle — it's him again. He's waiting for you.*

SEVERINE jumps up immediately and goes out. ANAIS takes her seat.

Medium shot of MARCEL seen from outside the window of the Pink Room. He is standing looking out, nervously picking his teeth with a match. SEVERINE opens the door and enters in the background. MARCEL whips round and walks towards her.

Medium shot of SEVERINE from inside the room. She smiles nervously at MARCEL and seems pleased to see him again. She comes towards him.

SEVERINE: *Hello, how are you?*

Ignoring her greeting, MARCEL goes over and kicks the door shut behind her.

MARCEL turning to face her furiously: *Where've you been? Why did you go away?*

SEVERINE nervously: *I had to leave Paris for a few days. I'll explain.*

MARCEL: *I'm going to explain as well . . . And leave my signature on you . . .* He walks past her towards camera.

Reverse angle shot of him as he quickly takes his belt off and walks towards her, threateningly. It is a large studded leather belt with a large copper buckle. Camera tracks out to include SEVERINE as he comes towards her.

SEVERINE: *Don't touch my face!*

---

\* Aeneas.
\*\* This is not heard in the film.

Looking at her wildly, MARCEL raises his belt to strike.

SEVERINE screams: *Don't touch me!* She covers her face with her arms. (Still on page 146)

Reverse angle close-up of SEVERINE. She takes the blow on the forearm (Still on page 146), then whips round, eyes blazing, and says to him:

SEVERINE: *If you start that again, I'll leave . . . And you won't see me again.*

Reverse angle medium close-up of MARCEL, with SEVERINE back to camera in the foreground. They confront each other in silence. SEVERINE seems very decided. MARCEL glares at her like a frustrated child.

MARCEL: *All right, this time . . .*

Camera pans as he walks across the room; he suddenly turns and lashes out with his belt at a picture of a naked woman on the wall. It shatters and falls to the floor. (Stills on page 146) He walks across the room, thrusting his hands petulantly in his pockets, staring at SEVERINE.

Reverse angle medium close-up of SEVERINE watching him intently. She smiles faintly and sits down on the end of the bed. Camera tilts with her. MARCEL appears and sits down beside her. He speaks to her almost beseechingly, all his rage spent.

MARCEL: *I've missed you . . . you know . . . I shouldn't tell you this, but I waited for you . . . Now I want to see more of you — at night as well.*

Camera tracks in on them slowly.

SEVERINE: *Isn't it enough for you that I come here every day?*

MARCEL: *No.*

SEVERINE: *But you know very well that I'm not free.*

MARCEL: *I don't give a damn.*

He kisses her, then falls back with her onto the bed.

Medium close-up of them on the bed, kissing. After a moment MARCEL draws away and says:

MARCEL: *I don't understand. You seem to like being with me . . .*

SEVERINE in a low voice: *I do, a lot. But it's not enough.*

MARCEL: *You love the other one?*

SEVERINE nods her head, without replying. MARCEL turns her face towards him. He cannot understand and says, annoyed:

MARCEL: *What do you come here for, then?*

SEVERINE with the greatest sincerity and sadness: *I don't know . . . They're two quite separate things . . .*

MARCEL leans forward and kisses her, interrupting what she is saying. Camera pans along their bodies as he crawls on top of her, and holds on their feet. MARCEL kicks off one of his boots and rubs his foot along her leg. His sock has a large hole in the heel. (Still on page 146)

Shot of the courtyard of the hospital where PIERRE works. Camera tracks out in front of PIERRE and SEVERINE as they come towards us. SEVERINE is not wearing the same clothes as in the preceding scene; it is not the same day. PIERRE has his arm round his wife and they are both laughing gaily. They look the picture of a happy couple and the clouds over their marriage seem to have disappeared.

PIERRE: *I'm dying of hunger . . . Where shall we lunch?*

SEVERINE: *No idea. We'll think about it on the way.*

They pause as they come up to a young MEDICAL STUDENT and PIERRE says to him:

PIEERE: *I shan't be long. I'll be back at three o'clock.*

MEDICAL STUDENT: *Right, sir.*

He goes off, and camera continues to track out in front of the couple as they walk.

PIERRE: *How you've changed . . . I can hardly recognize you . . . It's so nice to see you smile . . .*

SEVERINE: *I certainly feel much better.*

PIERRE: *I've never seen you like this. If only . . .*

SEVERINE: *What?*

PIERRE stops and looks at her.

PIERRE: *Oh, nothing . . . If only, one day, you had some good news to tell me . . .*

SEVERINE: *What are you talking about?*

PIERRE: *You know very well . . . What I want more than anything . . . a child.* (Still on page 147)

Camera holds on the two of them. SEVERINE freezes at the word ' child ' as though she is suddenly afraid. Sound of an ambulance siren off. PIERRE takes her hand and leads her out of shot.

Medium shot of the hospital entrance from the street. The ambulance drives in through the gateway as PIERRE and SEVERINE emerge. PIERRE notices something on the pavement near by and stops. SEVERINE goes off towards their car while camera pans left with PIERRE as he goes towards a hospital wheelchair, abandoned and empty on the pavement. He looks at it with a frown. He is puzzled and worried. (Still on page 147) SEVERINE comes up and asks him :

SEVERINE : *What are you looking at?*

PIERRE suddenly seems to wake up.

PIERRE : *Nothing . . . It's this machine . . . I was struck by it, I don't know why, it's funny . . .*

SEVERINE : *There's nothing funny about it . . .*

PIERRE : *No, you're quite right . . .*

Camera pans right as they go towards their car. SEVERINE gets into the driver's seat. PIERRE gets in with a last look at the wheelchair.

[On the landing at ANAIS'S, a man is standing with his back to camera, waiting for the door to open. We cannot see his face, but we can just see that he is wearing dark glasses.]*

Shot of the entrance hall at ANAIS'S seen through the curtained door of the living room. Camera moves across to show ANAIS talking to a man, whose face we cannot see. She seems very pleased to see him.

ANAIS : *Ah! You've come back! . . . I didn't recognize you. You'd forgotten me, hadn't you, you ungrateful devil? We haven't seen you for ages . . .* Looking him up and down. *You haven't changed. Still the same . . .* Pointing down the corridor : *First door on the right.*

The man turns and goes off. Camera tracks out as ANAIS

---

* This section did not appear in the version screened.

comes quickly towards the living room and comes in.

ANAIS happy: *Come on, girls, an old friend's back.*

There is no response from the room. Looking slightly disappointed, ANAIS says:

ANAIS with a sigh: *Well, come along . . . don't you want to have a look?*

MATHILDE goes out first, then CHARLOTTE, followed by SEVERINE. They all titivate before going towards the Pink Room. ANAIS follows them out, remarking:

ANAIS: *Oh yes, you're all lovely . . .*

Medium shot inside the Pink Room. PALLAS is making the bed. A voice in the room says:

VOICE off: *You flatter me.*

Camera tracks out to include the man we have just seen, standing in back view in the foreground as PALLAS comes up to him and says in her child-like voice:

PALLAS: *No, monsieur, I remember you very well, and sometimes I even dream of you.*

The man takes a step forward and says:

MAN: *I don't much care for that.*

He takes out a banknote and holds it out to PALLAS.

PALLAS: *Oh no, monsieur.*

MAN insisting: *Yes . . . Yes . . . to please me.*

PALLAS: *Thank you, monsieur.*

She takes the note, and camera pans left as she goes out of the door. At that moment ANAIS appears, followed by the three girls. The man addresses them from off-screen. He is very polite.

MAN off: *Good afternoon, ladies . . . Please sit down.*

CHARLOTTE: *Thank you, monsieur.*

ANAIS moves off to the right as she introduces the girls.

ANAIS: *This is Charlotte . . . Mathilde . . . and Belle de Jour.*

SEVERINE, who has been adjusting the sleeve of her dressing gown, looks up for the first time and stares at the man in amazement.

Medium shot of the man with MATHILDE and CHARLOTTE in the foreground.

MAN: *Belle de Jour?*

Camera zooms in on his face as he removes his dark glasses. It is HENRI HUSSON.

HUSSON : *An original name* . . .

HUSSON recognizes her. He is slightly surprised, but quickly recovers his sang-froid. Nothing gives away the fact that he knows SEVERINE.

Medium close-up of SEVERINE, gazing at HUSSON, petrified. She involuntarily takes a step backwards. She seems suddenly to have lost all her strength. She feels lost. But there is a perfectly harmless conversation going on around her. (Still on page 147)

ANAIS to HUSSON, off : *Perhaps you'd like some refreshment?*

HUSSON off : *Later, later* . . .

Medium shot of HUSSON. He seems to have all the time in the world. Camera pans with him as, taking off his coat, he walks round the room, looking about him.

HUSSON : *Nothing has changed at Anaïs's — the same curtains* . . . Smiling : *Still the same wide-open welcome* . . . He lifts one of the curtains and sniffs it, then adds casually : *What happened to that tigress you had here?*

ANAIS leaning against the end of the bed : *Ah!* She laughs . . . *I don't know* . . . *I haven't had any news.*

HUSSON : *The heating full on* . . .

ANAIS remembering : *And you haven't changed either.*

HUSSON throws down his coat and sits in an armchair.

HUSSON : *Well, well, the same armchair* . . . Reminiscently : *It was snowing* . . . To the girls : *Still the same special perfume* . . .

ANAIS : *Still Jasmin.* She comes round him. *You'll stay for a while, I hope?*

HUSSON : *All my life. I've always plenty of time to spare* . . . *Let's see* . . . (Still on page 147)

He looks carefully at the three girls. CHARLOTTE and MATHILDE stand expectantly in front of him. Throughout this conversation SEVERINE has been standing in the corner with her back to them, ignoring the proceedings. HUSSON comes to a decision and jerks his head in the direction of SEVERINE.

HUSSON : *I'd like to be alone with Belle de Jour.*

139

Charlotte and Mathilde leave the room immediately. Severine quickly turns round, as if by reflex, and goes towards the door, avoiding Husson's look, without knowing very well what she is doing. Anais goes towards her and stops her in the doorway.

Medium close-up of the two of them. Anais blocks Severine's path.

Severine : *No, no . . . I won't! . . .*

Anais, surprised, takes her by the arm.

Anais : *What do you think you're up to? Just you stay here!* To Husson reassuringly : *She's very sweet, but sometimes she gets a bit nervous.*

Defeated, Severine goes back towards the middle of the room. [Anais says to Husson as she goes out :

Anais : *See you later . . .]**

Medium shot of the room, with Husson sitting in back view in the foreground. As soon as she is alone with Husson and the door is closed, Severine rounds on him. She walks across the room and says bitterly :

Severine : *Are you pleased with yourself? Don't tell me it's an accident! You knew I was here!*

Husson sincerely : *You're wrong.*

Severine turns to face him. Her face has become hard, violent and full of hate. She breaks out :

Severine : *It's your fault! You gave me this address!*

Husson getting up and moving towards her : *I'm telling you you're wrong.*

Husson has made a vague gesture (he does not remember) and continues to look at Severine with intense curiosity. His smile has gone. Severine backs towards the window.

Severine half screaming, at the end of her tether : *If you come near me, I'll scream, I'll shout to the people in the street, I'll throw myself out of the window!*

Husson does not move. Camera pans, cutting out Severine, as he walks round the other side of the bed, tries the springs and asks calmly :

---

* This piece of dialogue was not heard in the version screened.

Husson : *Is that your bed?* (Still on page 147)
Severine reappearing : *You disgust me, I've already told you
. . .* Facing him across the bed, she shouts at him violently :
*Yes, it's my bed! Is there anything else you want to know?*

Husson does not reply directly. He looks at her closely,
then comes towards camera and says in a low voice :
Husson : *You like to be humiliated . . . I don't . . .*

Severine has become a little calmer. She seems to be
hesitating before saying something to Husson, then she
makes up her mind.
Severine : *Don't say anything to Pierre!*
Husson without looking at her : *Pierre?* A pause. Rather at a
loss, he adds : *I admire him more and more.*

Severine comes slowly towards him, now almost desperate, pleading.
Severine : *Don't say anything to him, please! Try to understand, at least! I'm completely lost. Everything happens in
spite of me. I can't do anything about it, I can't resist it . . .
I know that I'll have to pay one day for everything I've done
. . . But I couldn't live without it . . .*

Medium close-up of Severine. She points to the bed and
says defiantly :
Severine : *Anyway, do what you want with me . . .*

Camera pans as she goes off and Husson appears in back
view. Husson has changed his attitude. He has become
hard and rather mocking.
Husson : *Not now, anyway. You see, what attracted me
about you . . . I don't know, I suppose it was your virtue
. . .* He laughs and sits down on the end of the bed facing us.
*All that has changed . . . I've got principles, I'm not like
you.* He gets up again and camera pans to include Severine
as he goes towards her. *But I shall say nothing to Pierre,
naturally . . . But I have friends who would be delighted to
know you're here. I could send you some customers.* A pause.
Husson seems a fraction embarrassed. He folds his arms and
says : *You must excuse my sudden lack of interest. I really
don't feel like it.* He gives a nervous laugh. *Another day,
perhaps. I don't want to waste your time.*

Camera pans as he walks across the room to pick up his

coat. Then he comes back past SEVERINE, who sits down in the armchair at the end of the bed. Just before going out he throws a couple of banknotes down on the table near the door.

HUSSON: *This is not for you. You can buy Pierre some chocolates, from me . . . Goodbye.*

He goes out, and camera moves in to medium close-up of SEVERINE sitting dejectedly in the armchair, in back view, her head in her hands.

It is early morning. We are in the Bois de Boulogne, very near the clearing where the first sequence took place. It very soon becomes evident that a duel is about to take place. Camera pans with a berline drawn by two black horses as it comes along a quiet avenue, passes the landau which we have seen before, and goes off. Camera holds on the landau. Several people, dressed in black, get out. There are four people, apart from the COACHMAN and FOOTMAN, who remain with the carriage. They are all dressed in the styles of 1880. We know one of them: PIERRE. They move away from the carriage and go towards a clearing. Camera pans to show the berline halted in the background with a similar party beside it, one of whom is HUSSON. PIERRE passes with his seconds and the two parties raise their top hats in greeting.

High angle medium close-up of a case containing duelling pistols. One of the seconds is holding a pistol, ladling powder into the barrel. (Still on page 148)

High angle medium close-up: a little way away, the doctor on duty is laying out a number of instruments on a white cloth spread on the grass (tweezers, surgical knife, scissors and a probe), as well as a bottle of alcohol, cotton-wool and gauze. (Still on page 148)

Resume on the duelling pistols. The SECOND inserts a bullet into the barrel of the one he is loading.

[The REFEREE of the duel calls the two contestants, PIERRE and HUSSON, to him, and puts them back to back. PIERRE and HUSSON turn up the lapels of their frock-coats and button them. The seconds come up to give them their guns.]*

Medium shot of the two contestants standing back to back, holding their guns, with the REFEREE a little way away and the seconds in the background. PIERRE is calm and looks indifferent, very much in control of himself. In contrast, HUSSON is breathing heavily and perspiring slightly. He is afraid. The REFEREE, when they are ready, says to them:

REFEREE: *Are you set? . . . March!* (Still on page 148)

Camera tracks out as PIERRE and HUSSON, their backs to one another, each takes four steps across the clearing, in opposite directions. When they have finished their steps, the REFEREE says to them in a louder voice:

REFEREE: *Get ready!*

They raise their pistols to shoulder height.

REFEREE: *Fire!*

They turn round to face each other.

Medium close-up of HUSSON as he turns, takes aim and fires.

Low angle medium close-up of PIERRE, who aims carefully and fires. (Still on page 148) A dog barks in the distance. PIERRE lowers his pistol. Suddenly his gaze becomes fixed on something, some distance away. [He points and shouts:

PIERRE horrified: *Look!*

Everyone turns round to look in the direction in which PIERRE is pointing.]*

Medium shot of what he sees: dressed in the same clothes which she wore during the first sequence, SEVERINE is seen tied to a tree.** Her body seems lifeless, and is elaborately bound to the tree-trunk by a rope. She does not move. There is a loud crashing of waves, off, as camera tracks in towards her and we see that her eyes are open, but lifeless. She is not breathing. She has been hit by a bullet in the temple and a trickle of blood is running down her face. PIERRE comes up. (Still on page

---

* This section did not appear in the version screened.
** Buñuel's note: ' The same tree.'

148) He kisses her passionately, then puts his hand up to her temple and touches it. He looks at the blood on his hand, then kisses her again. Camera tracks in to medium close-up of their faces.

*[Interior shot of the bathroom at ANAIS'S. ANAIS has just washed her hair and is finishing drying it, with the help of young CATHERINE.

ANAIS : *Put that away and give me the brush . . .*

CATHERINE : *They make fun of me at school, Godmother.*

ANAIS : *Why?*

She takes the brush from CATHERINE and starts to brush her hair, while CATHERINE switches the dryer off and starts to put it away.

CATHERINE : *Because my mummy works here. And the supervisor said that, if I continue, I shall work here too.*

ANAIS : *Your supervisor is an idiot.*]

Long shot of the corridor at ANAIS'S. SEVERINE passes PALLAS and hurries towards camera, which tracks out in front of her to show ANAIS and CATHERINE standing in back view in the bathroom. SEVERINE stops in the doorway of the bathroom and ANAIS, rather surprised, asks her :

ANAIS : *What . . . has he gone already?*

SEVERINE : *Yes . . . Can I speak to you?*

She goes into the adjoining Pink Room. ANAIS turns towards CATHERINE and motions to her to go, saying quietly to her :

ANAIS : *That's all for now.*

She pats CATHERINE on the head and CATHERINE goes off down the corridor. ANAIS finishes brushing her hair, and camera follows as she goes through the door into the Pink Room, where SEVERINE is waiting for her. SEVERINE says, very quickly :

SEVERINE : *I must leave . . .*

ANAIS : *When?*

---

* The following sequence at Anaïs's precedes the duel scene in the original script; the section in square brackets did not appear in the version screened.

144

SEVERINE : *Now.*

ANAIS : *But you'll come back?*

SEVERINE : *No, definitely not.*

ANAIS very displeased : *What? But . . . You could have told me before!* She walks past SEVERINE into the room. *Aren't you all right here?*

SEVERINE : *Yes, perfectly all right. But . . .*

ANAIS interrupting her : *Ah! I understand.*

High angle medium close-up of ANAIS as she sits down in the corner of the room.

ANAIS : *It's Marcel?* SEVERINE does not answer. *He came three minutes ago. Furious. He nearly went in to your room . . .* She gazes reflectively into space and says : *There's something fishy there . . .* Looking at SEVERINE : *He's become too demanding, I suppose? He wants you for himself alone, day and night?*

Reverse angle medium close-up of SEVERINE. She nods.

SEVERINE : *Yes.*

Camera follows her as she walks across the room, holding a cigarette.

ANAIS off : *It's always the same with men . . .* She comes into frame and camera pans to follow her, losing SEVERINE. She says resignedly : *You're quite right to leave. One of these days there could be trouble . . .* She goes towards SEVERINE. *But I'll be sorry to see you go . . . Women like you . . .* She adds, almost tenderly : *We really got on well together, didn't we?*

SEVERINE turning to face her : *Yes, that's true.*

ANAIS : *Let me know how you're getting on, if you can. Give me a ring now and again . . . I'd like that . . . Do you have an address, where no one would know if I . . . ?*

SEVERINE interrupting firmly : *No.*

ANAIS rebuffed : *Oh well, too bad . . . What am I supposed to say, then?*

SEVERINE throws away her cigarette, turns and suddenly draws ANAIS to her. ANAIS gazes at her coldly. SEVERINE tries to kiss her, but ANAIS turns her face away. (Still on page 149) SEVERINE kisses her on the neck, then hurries off. ANAIS gazes after her.

Medium shot of the entrance to Number 11. SEVERINE comes out of the block, wearing her dark glasses, looks from side to side and quickly walks away along the pavement.

Long shot of the entrance from the other side of the square. As SEVERINE comes out, a man wearing a fawn raincoat and trilby hat — who has apparently been watching the entrance — turns to face camera. It is HIPPOLYTE. He waits for a moment, then camera pans left and tracks after him as he walks across the square. SEVERINE quickly turns the corner of the street. HIPPO-LYTE walks about a dozen yards behind, shadowing her. We lose them both among the passers-by.

The scene changes to the drawing room of SEVERINE'S apartment. It is afternoon. PIERRE is at the hospital, as usual. SEVERINE, who no longer goes to ANAIS'S, is alone. Camera follows her across the room as she picks up a tumbler and soda siphon from the drinks trolley and goes to sit down on the sofa. She undoes a parcel which contains a pair of new shoes. She takes one of the shoes and examines it, bending it to try it for suppleness. Just then the MAID comes into the drawing room and says to her:

MAID : *Madame . . . There's a gentleman to see you . . .*

SEVERINE surprised : *Me?*

MAID : *Yes, madame.*

SEVERINE : *Who is it? Do you know him?*

MAID : *I don't know . . . but he says that it's urgent.*

The MAID goes off and camera pans as the sliding door behind SEVERINE is suddenly flung open. MARCEL enters, carrying his cane and coat. SEVERINE looks round, recognizes MARCEL and leaps to her feet, dropping the shoes.

Medium close-up of MARCEL.

MARCEL : *Good afternoon.*

He looks at SEVERINE sardonically, tosses his cane in the air and catches it and moves towards her, out of shot. At this moment the MAID appears in the open doorway and stares after MARCEL with a mixture of amazement and alarm. Camera tracks in on her as SEVERINE speaks off.

SEVERINE to MARCEL off : *Have you brought the catalogue?*
MARCEL off : *Yes, madame.*
SEVERINE off : *Well* . . . Dismissing the MAID : *Thank you, Maria.*

> The MAID slides the doors shut in front of her.
> Medium shot of MARCEL standing by the sofa. After casting a glance at the door he says ironically :

MARCEL : *Very neat, asking for a catalogue.*

> He throws his coat down on the sofa. Camera moves with him as he begins to walk round the room. He looks at the furniture, the ornaments and the paintings. He seems to appreciate their quality. Finally he stops in the middle of the drawing room and, looking around him and nodding his head admiringly, says :

MARCEL : *Not a bad sort of place you've got here* . . .

> SEVERINE comes round to face him, panic-stricken.

SEVERINE : *What are you doing here? You're crazy!*

> MARCEL continues to stroll nonchalantly around the room, swinging his cane.

MARCEL : *Since you'd vanished from Anaïs's* . . . *I thought to myself* . . . *well, let's go and pay her a little visit* . . . *and see how she's getting on* . . .

> As he finishes, cut to a medium close-up of a photograph of PIERRE standing on a piano with a lacquered case. MARCEL notices the photograph of PIERRE and picks it up.

SEVERINE nervously, off : *How did you find* . . . *?*
MARCEL casually, looking at the photograph : *Child's play. This your husband?*

> SEVERINE does not reply. MARCEL looks at the photograph carefully and says :

MARCEL : *Good-looking guy* . . .

> Medium close-up of MARCEL from behind.

MARCEL : *Friendly* . . . *A lot better than me, I'm sure.*

> He throws the photograph down on the piano and walks across the room again. Camera pans as SEVERINE rushes across to bar his way and says desperately :

SEVERINE : *Will you please go away.*

> MARCEL fends her off with his cane, and camera pans as

155

he walks on again. His even voice does not really hide the threat in it:

MARCEL : *Don't worry . . . I won't make a fuss . . . I only wanted to know why you had left . . . That's all.*

SEVERINE, who is now off-screen, does not reply. MARCEL, who is losing his patience, suddenly turns and bawls at her.

MARCEL angrily : *You hear?*

SEVERINE rushes up to him and, dropping her voice, says :

SEVERINE : *Don't shout . . . The maid will hear . . .* She drops her voice even further and says beseechingly : *You must go . . . He'll be back soon . . .*

MARCEL becoming calmer : *I've only just got here and you want me to go already.*

His voice is normal. In contrast, SEVERINE is speaking in a very low voice. Her fear grows continually throughout the scene, and MARCEL's apparent indifference only makes her more apprehensive.

SEVERINE : *What do you want?*

MARCEL : *I want to see you again.*

SEVERINE angrily, moving out of shot: *No, it's impossible. I've told you I'll never go back there again.*

Camera pans as MARCEL walks swiftly across the room past SEVERINE and stops by the sofa.

Medium close-up of MARCEL; he raises his cane threateningly at SEVERINE and says :

MARCEL : *I'll give you three days. Find an excuse . . . It doesn't matter what. I'll be waiting for you at the Hotel du Bois in the Rue Fromentin. You'll stay all night with me.*

A closer shot of MARCEL as he turns to go.

SEVERINE off : *Impossible.*

MARCEL turns very slowly towards her. Camera pans to include her standing by the window.

MARCEL : *Very well . . . I'll wait for him.*

He walks over to the second sofa, elaborately dusts off the seat and sits down.

MARCEL with emphasis : *I shall have a lot to tell him.*

SEVERINE has followed him and stands a little way away.

SEVERINE anxiously : *No, you wouldn't do that . . .*

MARCEL : *Yes I will. I didn't want it to come to that . . .*
*But since you force me to . . .*

> SEVERINE moves a little closer to him and sits down on
> the arm of an armchair. She thinks for a moment, then
> tries to push the danger further away. (Still on page 149)

SEVERINE looking completely beaten : *Perhaps it's just as well
. . . I've decided to tell him everything anyway.*

MARCEL unbelieving : *Honestly?*

SEVERINE in a low voice : *He'd have got to know sooner or
later. One of our friends found me there .      And I want to
get this off my mind once and for all . . .*

> She gets up and goes out of shot. Camera pans towards
> MARCEL, who does not believe a word of what she is
> saying. Leaning forward, he picks up the tumbler which
> is on the table in front of him and reaches for the soda
> siphon.

MARCEL : *That's fine, then. Let's wait for him together.*

> Medium close-up of SEVERINE. Camera pans with her as
> she goes across towards the dining room.

MARCEL off : *We'll tell him the story together . . .* We hear
the hiss of the soda siphon . . . *I don't mind.*

> At these words SEVERINE whips round to face him. She
> seems almost in tears.
> Low angle medium close-up of MARCEL. He puts the
> soda siphon down with a self-satisfied expression. (Still
> on page 149)
> Resume on SEVERINE. She walks to and fro, looking
> desperate. Camera pans with her as she suddenly hurries
> towards MARCEL and kneels down beside him, putting
> her hand on his arm.

SEVERINE beseechingly : *Please, please, go away . . . He'll be
here any minute.*

> MARCEL ponders for a moment, clutching his glass. He
> looks at her and what he sees in her face seems to con-
> vince him. He gets up, taking her by the wrist, and
> camera tilts up with them. She kisses him and they stand
> for a moment holding each other. The expression on
> his face has changed. There is nothing threatening or
> mocking in it. He has become serious and his look has

softened. (Still on page 149)

MARCEL : *All right . . . there's no need to be afraid . . . I'll go. I didn't believe you, but I'm beginning to understand.*

Medium shot of MARCEL as he walks across to the piano and picks up the photograph of PIERRE.

MARCEL : *That's the obstacle . . .* He throws down the photograph and walks off.

Reverse angle medium shot as MARCEL strides across the room to the sliding doors, grabbing his coat from the sofa on the way. He slides open one of the doors, turns and pauses theatrically.

MARCEL : *See you soon . . . Séverine.*

He crosses the corridor and goes out through the front door. SEVERINE hurries into shot and out into the corridor, looking to and fro to make sure that the MAID is not there. A clock strikes as she comes back into the drawing room, biting her nails. She sits on the arm of the sofa, looking dazed. Camera pans with her as she gets up and walks up and down nervously, looking completely lost.

Medium shot of the street outside SEVERINE'S flat. (Still on page 149) MARCEL strides out of the apartment block and camera follows him as he comes across to the other side of the street where HIPPOLYTE is waiting, sitting at the wheel of a car. MARCEL opens the passenger door, looks around him for a moment and then gets in. Camera pans across the front of the car.

Medium close-up of HIPPOLYTE and MARCEL seen through the side window of the car. HIPPOLYTE is at the wheel.

HIPPOLYTE : *Did you see her?*

MARCEL : *Yes.* Brutally : *Leave me the car.*

HIPPOLYTE surprised : *To go where?*

MARCEL : *I need it. Give me the car and clear off.*

A pause. HIPPOLYTE looks at MARCEL anxiously.

HIPPOLYTE very quietly : *What are you cooking up now?*

MARCEL, who is obviously in a state of great tension, plunges his hand in his pocket and takes out a gun which he suddenly points at HIPPOLYTE.

MARCEL : *I said clear off.*

The two men exchange looks. HIPPOLYTE is not at all frightened by the gun, but he does look rather weary.

HIPPOLYTE : *This time, kid, you've seen the last of me.*

Jamming his cigar butt into his mouth, he opens the door and gets out. Camera tracks in on MARCEL as he puts down the gun and sits looking out through the windscreen, brooding.

We are back in the drawing room in SEVERINE'S apartment. Camera pans with the MAID as she enters the room and goes across to the sofa, hesitates, and picks up the shoe box which SEVERINE dropped earlier. Camera moves with her as she goes out of the room, and pans slowly back to the sofa.

[MAID : *Shall I put them away, or will Madame be wearing them?*

SEVERINE : *Put them away.*

MAID : *Yes, madame.*]*

Suddenly, three gunshots are heard in quick succession from the street outside. SEVERINE, who has evidently been lying down on the sofa, now rises into view as she sits up. Camera pans as she walks quickly across to the french windows, draws aside the net curtains and looks out. She then opens the window and hurries out onto the balcony.

Medium shot of SEVERINE from the side as she runs to the edge of the balcony and looks over into the street. Camera swoops round and down to show what she sees : MARCEL'S car draws away from the kerb and accelerates up the street. Camera follows it for a moment, then tilts down to show a figure sprawled on the pavement directly below the balcony. Passers-by run up and bend over the figure. (Still on page 150)

Shot through the windscreen of the car, from the driver's seat, as it moves very fast up the street.

Reverse angle medium close-up of MARCEL at the wheel, driving with a feverish expression. He glances anxiously behind him.

---

* This section of dialogue does not occur in the film.

High angle medium shot panning with the car as it hurtles round one corner after another, tyres screaming. Resume on MARCEL, spinning the wheel, wild-eyed. He gets the car straight again and pushes his thumb nervously against his gold teeth, sucking in his cheeks.

Long shot of a street. Another car pulls away from the kerb as MARCEL's car races towards camera. MARCEL brakes too late and hits the other car squarely in the side.

Long shot of a POLICEMAN checking a lorry driver's licence with the number plate. He whips round at the sound of the crash. Camera pans as he hurriedly gives the driver back his licence then walks off.

Medium close-up of MARCEL in the driver's seat trying furiously to open his door. It is jammed. He slides across and gets out of the passenger door. Camera pans as he starts to hurry off up the street only to be met by the driver of the other car, who grabs him by the lapels and starts yelling at him furiously. MARCEL grapples with him for a moment and then flings him to the ground. (Still on page 150) Pan as he rushes off up the street only to find his exit blocked by the POLICEMAN. He completely loses his head and dashes back towards the cars. The POLICEMAN gives chase, blowing his whistle.

Long shot from the other end of the street. MARCEL dashes back past the crashed cars, coming towards camera, which pans slightly left as he hides round a corner and pulls out his gun. The POLICEMAN rushes up in the background. MARCEL leans round the corner and fires twice (Still on page 150), then runs off as the POLICEMAN takes refuge behind a parked car.

High angle medium close-up of the POLICEMAN crouching down beside the car. He raises his gun, aims carefully and fires. (Still on page 150)

Long shot of the street. MARCEL rushes away from camera as the POLICEMAN fires a second time. MARCEL stops, turns and aims — but his gun is empty. (Still on page 150) The POLICEMAN fires a third time. MARCEL clutches his stomach and falls to the ground, dropping his gun. He rolls over, dead.

We are inside a hospital corridor. At first camera focuses on an empty stretcher trolley, then tilts up as a male nurse wheels it slowly up the corridor. Several surgeons, whom we have seen earlier in the hospital courtyard (among them PROFESSOR HENRI, the chief surgeon), are coming in the opposite direction.

[PROFESSOR HENRI looking at the trolley: *Poor Sérizy . . . Who'd have thought that some day . . .?*]*

PROFESSOR HENRI, who seems tired, suddenly sees a young MEDICAL STUDENT, a friend of PIERRE's, who is waiting in the corridor. He takes a couple of steps towards him and asks:

PROFESSOR HENRI: *Well, any news?*

MEDICAL STUDENT: *The murderer is dead and the police are baffled . . . They say he got the wrong man, or else he was mad . . .*

PROFESSOR HENRI: *Has he been identified?*

MEDICAL STUDENT: *Some crook . . . Apparently he's killed before . . .*

The PROFESSOR does not seem to be able to understand the relationship which might exist between MARCEL and PIERRE.

PROFESSOR HENRI: *It's very strange . . .*

MEDICAL STUDENT: *And how's Sérizy?*

Camera starts to track out in front of the group as they walk on down the corridor. The PROFESSOR's expression does not inspire confidence.

PROFESSOR HENRI: *It's too early to say.*

The MEDICAL STUDENT adds, with a jerk of his head:

MEDICAL STUDENT: *His wife's in the waiting room.*

Camera pans left with the group as PROFESSOR HENRI leads them round a corner and through some plastic swing doors. Doctors and nurses hurry to and fro.

Low angle medium close-up, tracking with PROFESSOR HENRI as he arrives at the door of the waiting room followed by two of his colleagues. He looks in through the door but does not find what he is looking for. As he

---

* This section of dialogue was not heard in the version screened.

turns away from the door, SEVERINE comes up to him and looks at him anxiously. The PROFESSOR puts a reassuring arm round her and camera follows as they take a few steps to the right, where RENEE is also waiting.

SEVERINE : *How is he?*

PROFESSOR HENRI : *Too early to say. But he'll live, so don't worry.*

SEVERINE : *Can I see him?*

PROFESSOR HENRI : *No, I'm sorry. He's still in a coma. Perhaps tomorrow . . . You should go back home, Madame Sérizy . . . And try to rest . . . We'll keep you informed every hour, I promise you . . .*

SEVERINE : *Thank you.*

He pats her on the shoulder and says :

PROFESSOR HENRI : *Don't worry.*

He goes off, and camera tracks in as RENEE takes her by the arm.

RENEE : *Come on, I'll come with you.*

Camera pans to show them from behind as they go out through the entrance hall of the hospital.

Long shot as camera pans obliquely across the façade of the apartment block where SEVERINE and PIERRE live. Moving across in superimposition, we see a pattern of trees against a blue sky. It is autumn and their leaves are golden brown. Sound of pouring rain.

Medium close-up of SEVERINE as she looks through the window at the rain. (Still on page 151) Seen dimly through the rain-soaked window, the MAID comes into the room, carrying a tray. SEVERINE turns and says something to her, then draws the net curtains as the MAID disappears from sight.

General shot of the drawing room with the dining room in the background. The MAID puts the tray down on a table by the drinks trolley. On the tray is a glass, some granulated sugar and a lemon cut in half. She puts a decanter of water on the tray from the drinks trolley and goes off. SEVERINE, who has appeared from the foreground, puts a small spoonful of sugar in the glass. Then

162

she picks up the tray and camera pans with her as she carries it across to the other side of the room and puts it down on a low table in front of PIERRE, who is seated in a wheelchair wearing a dressing gown (only the lower half of his body can be seen). Camera follows her over to the fireplace. She stokes the fire, talking to PIERRE, who is not seen.

SEVERINE : *I've sent Maria to get the newspapers. I know what articles you're interested in. I'll read them to you. She's very kind, Maria. Very good at her job. She thinks a lot of you* . . .

Camera pans as she goes across to PIERRE, whom we now see. He is sitting absolutely stiff, in an invalid chair. His face has become thin and gaunt. He is completely paralysed, and wears dark glasses. His hands lie motionless in his lap. SEVERINE leans towards him, moves him forward and adjusts his pillow.

SEVERINE : *Everyone is asking after you.* She kisses him on the cheek and goes round behind him. *You're much better, you know. The Professor is very optimistic.*

Camera pans right, cutting out PIERRE, as SEVERINE goes and sits down in a chair close to him. She takes up her embroidery and starts work, looking at PIERRE from time to time, kindly and concerned. She seems calm and peaceful. As she goes on talking we realize that, in addition to being paralysed and possibly blind, PIERRE also cannot speak.

SEVERINE : *You don't realize it but you're making great progress. Your eyes especially. It's funny, since you* . . . She falters . . . *you had* . . . *your accident* . . . *I haven't had any more dreams* . . . Silence. She looks up.

High angle medium close-up of PIERRE sitting motionless in the wheelchair. Camera zooms in on him as SEVERINE says, off :

SEVERINE : *I think it's time* . . . *I'll give you your drops.*

Medium shot of the tray standing on the table in front of the fireplace. SEVERINE kneels down beside it, picks up a small bottle of medicine and shakes several drops of it into the glass, which has been half filled with water. She stirs the contents of the glass, and camera tilts up as she takes it across to PIERRE. She raises his head by the chin and slowly pours the medicine between his lips. (Still on page 151) The MAID interrupts off-screen and says:

MAID : *It's Monsieur Husson, madame. He would like to see Monsieur.*

SEVERINE jumps slightly. She gives PIERRE another drop of medicine and then says :

SEVERINE : *I'm coming.*

Camera pans with her as she deposits the glass on the mantelpiece and leaves the drawing room.

Medium shot of PIERRE's study. SEVERINE enters from the drawing room in the background. Camera tracks in slightly as HUSSON walks towards her from the foreground. He is very correct and polite with her, but without showing any excessive friendliness.

HUSSON : *Good afternoon, Séverine . . . I'm sorry to disturb you.*

SEVERINE : *Do you want to see Pierre?*

HUSSON : *For a moment, yes.*

SEVERINE seems very uncomfortable. As she continues, she walks nervously around the room. Camera pans slightly to keep her in frame.

SEVERINE : *You know that he still can't speak, he's . . .*

HUSSON taking off his gloves : *I know . . . I'm sorry that I didn't come before. You know how much I admire Pierre — but I've been away. That's a pretty dress . . .* He walks round to inspect her . . . *just like a precocious schoolgirl . . .*

Camera pans with SEVERINE as she walks across in front of him. She says anxiously :

SEVERINE : *What do you want to say to Pierre?*

HUSSON : *Everything I know about you.* (Still on page 151)

SEVERINE gazes at him, stunned, and says in a whisper :

SEVERINE : *What?*

HUSSON sits down, laying a hand on her arm. He looks up at SEVERINE and says with perfect sincerity :

HUSSON lowering his voice : *You see, now he's paralysed he feels he's entirely dependent on you.*

He looks down as if slightly embarrassed about what he

164

is going to say next. Looking up, he continues:

HUSSON: *He's giving you a lot of trouble and he's ashamed of it, because he thinks you're pure. That's why I want to speak to him . . . tell him everything.*

SEVERINE bows her head without replying.

HUSSON: *I shall certainly hurt him . . . But at the same time perhaps I shall be helping him . . .* He laughs cheerfully . . . *After that, who could accuse me of being cruel?* He puts his hand on her arm, gets up and says gently: *Please show me in . . .*

SEVERINE looks up at him and says:

SEVERINE: *He's in there.*

HUSSON goes across the study to the door and pauses before opening it.

HUSSON: *Do you want to be present?*

SEVERINE says nothing. After a moment HUSSON goes into the drawing room, calling out heartily:

HUSSON off: *Hello, Pierre . . .* [*It's terrible weather outside . . . Raining, cold, winter's not far away . . .*]*

SEVERINE closes the door behind him and stays alone in the study. She looks bewildered.

High angle medium shot of the sofa in the study. SEVERINE appears and sits down on it, nervously twisting her fingers. Finally she gets up and goes out through the door into the hall. A clock chimes five o'clock somewhere in the apartment.

Shot from ground level, tracking with SEVERINE's feet as she walks nervously along the corridor. Camera tilts up to show her hand as she runs it along the edge of a marble side-table. She is obviously very tense. (Still on page 151)

Medium close-up of SEVERINE as she walks aimlessly along by a frosted glass door somewhere in the apartment.

[Shot of the kitchen in the apartment. The MAID, who is busy in the kitchen, sees SEVERINE come in. SEVERINE, who is clearly thinking of something else, takes an orange

---

* This piece of dialogue is not heard in the film.

and a knife, as if she were going to cut up the fruit. Then she sees a glass beside her. She takes the glass and starts wiping it mechanically with a dishcloth.]*

Long shot of the hall. HUSSON slides open the doors from the drawing room and comes out. Without saying a word he turns, takes a last look at PIERRE and closes the doors again. He comes towards camera, looking for SEVERINE, but cannot see her. He slings his scarf round his neck, and camera pans round to show the front door as he walks briskly out, slamming it behind him.

Medium close-up of SEVERINE as she comes nervously in through the door of the drawing room. Camera pans with her as she walks past PIERRE, who is still sitting motionless as before. She gazes at him, drawn by a certain feeling of curiosity. Camera continues to follow her as she slowly walks towards him. She says in a low whisper :

SEVERINE : *Pierre?*

Camera pans across to medium close-up of PIERRE's face; tears are flowing down his cheeks from behind his dark glasses. (Still on page 151)

High angle shot of SEVERINE's embroidery lying on a chair. Camera tilts up and pans across as she picks it up and goes to the sofa. She sits down and tries to start work again, but she has not got the strength. The needle slips between her fingers and falls. Camera tracks in as she leans back on the sofa and remains motionless for a moment. (Still on page 152)

Medium close-up of PIERRE. Camera tracks out to show him still in the same position, stiff-necked, sitting silently in the wheelchair.

Another shot of PIERRE, from above. Camera tilts down to show his hands lying motionless in his lap. (Still on page 152)

Medium close-up of him from below. A tear glistens on his cheek.

Medium close-up of SEVERINE. She looks up at him tenderly, then suddenly leans forward, surprised. (Still

---

* This section, taken from the original script, is replaced in the film by the two shots which precede it here.

on page 152) We hear the sound of cow-bells and a thunder of hooves off. SEVERINE's eyes light up.

Medium close-up of PIERRE. He has taken off his dark glasses. He sits up in the wheelchair, smiles at SEVERINE and says:

PIERRE: *What are you thinking about, Séverine?* (Still on page 152)

Resume on SEVERINE. She leans forward, smiling, and says:

SEVERINE: *I was thinking of you, Pierre.*

Medium shot of the room. PIERRE sits in the background by the window with SEVERINE facing him, back to camera, in the foreground. As the scene progresses, the noise of bells and hooves gets louder and is accompanied by the mewing of a cat.

PIERRE: *I'm thirsty.*

As if nothing was the matter, PIERRE gets up from the wheelchair, flinging aside the blanket which covers his knees. Camera pans as he strides across to the drinks trolley in the dining room and picks up a whisky decanter and a glass. SEVERINE follows him, and camera tracks in on the two of them. He pours some whisky into the glass and hands it to SEVERINE, who asks him in a very ordinary, very friendly voice:

SEVERINE: *Do you want me to ask for some ice?*

PIERRE kindly, pouring a glass for himself: *No, no, don't bother* . . . Putting down the decanter, he says: *I didn't tell you* . . . *I think I may be able to have a fortnight off in February, like last year.*

SEVERINE happy: *Shall we go to the mountains?*

PIERRE: *If you'd like that.*

SEVERINE: *Oh, yes* . . .

Medium close-up of the two of them standing under the chandelier. They raise their glasses. (Still on page 152) PIERRE is about to drink when SEVERINE takes his glass from him and puts it down, together with hers, on the drinks trolley. She comes towards him and he kisses her on the forehead. They stand holding one another in their arms. Just then the sound of cow-bells and hooves fades away, to be replaced by that of the bells on the harness of the landau. (Still on page 152) SEVERINE starts, looks up at PIERRE and says:

SEVERINE : *Do you hear that?*

Camera pans slightly as she goes across to the french window in the background, opens it and goes out onto the balcony. The noise of the landau gets louder. PIERRE picks up his glass from the trolley and drinks, watching her.

Medium close-up of SEVERINE against a background of trees as she stands looking down at the landau below. (Still on page 152)

High angle long shot of the avenue in the Bois de Boulogne seen at the beginning of the film. It is autumn and the ground is strewn with dry leaves. The noise of the harness bells becomes very loud as the landau comes towards camera, drawn by the horses and driven by the liveried COACHMAN with the FOOTMAN beside him. As it passes we see that it is empty. (Still on page 152) The words THE END appear, then disappear, and the camera holds for a long time on the carpet of dry leaves on the ground as the sound of harness bells mingles with the roar of traffic.